MW00467054

HI MOM, SEND SHEEP!

HI MOM, SEND SHEEP!

MY LIFE AS THE
COYOTE AND AFTER

Tim Derk

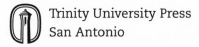

Trinity University Press
San Antonio

Published by Trinity University Press
San Antonio, Texas 78212

Jacket design by DJ Stout and Julie Savasky,
    Pentagram, Austin
Book design by BookMatters, Berkeley

♾ The paper used in this publication meets the
minimum requirements of the American National
Standard for Information Sciences—Permanence of
Paper for Printed Library Materials, ANSI Z39.48-1992.

Library of Congress Cataloging-in-Publication Data
Derk, Tim, 1957– .
Hi mom, send sheep! : my life as the Coyote and after /
Tim Derk.
    p.   cm.
SUMMARY: "The story of Tim Derk, who performed as
the Coyote, the mascot for the NBA San Antonio Spurs
basketball team, until his life and career were changed
following a massive stroke"—Provided by publisher.
  ISBN-13: 978-1-59534-025-2 (hardcover : alk. paper)
  ISBN-10: 1-59534-025-4 (hardcover : alk. paper)
1. Derk, Tim, 1957–   2. Sports team mascots—United
States—Biography.   3. San Antonio Spurs (Basketball
team)   4. Cerebrovascular disease—United States—
Biography.   I. Title.
GV714.5.D46   2006
796.323'6409764351—dc22   2006022788

PRINTED IN CANADA

10   09   08   07   06   /   5   4   3   2   1

This book is for my family and all those who have put up with my antics over the years. You know who you are. There are not enough poignant words to express my gratitude to you. I wish I had a nickel for each time you were patient with me and said, "I admire your courage but question your judgment."

I dedicate this book, too, to those who are peculiarly unique in the way they live in the world. I salute all of you who colored outside the lines in grade school—something that drove the nuns mad when I did it. I tip my hat to anyone who just can't sit still (I sure can't); to anyone working on making affordable soft bathtubs for the elderly; to those, like me, who are creatively colorful in their language and sometimes get in trouble for it; to Dick Van Dyke for his physical comedy; to those who think a child's laughter is the best music; to those who do push-ups until they can't do any more—and then do ten more; to the person who invented TiVo; to those who have prayed that their children might outlive them; to those who think talking animals seem perfectly feasible; and to those who might have plenty of regrets, but attempting something new is not one of them.

Whatever you do, do it with all your might. Work at it, early and late, in season and out of season, not leaving a stone unturned, and never deferring for a single hour that which can be done just as well now.

P. T. Barnum

Contents

Photo section follows page 78

Foreword

I have known Tim Derk for many years, and he has never ceased to amaze me. With his endless energy and boundless wit, he showed his God-given gift to entertain, game after game. You might think it would become old hat, perhaps even routine, after a few years, but nothing about Tim has ever been routine.

As a rookie, I watched as he worked in the South Texas sun, running from appearance to appearance, making children and adults happy, and converting new Spurs fans. Back then, he was the most popular Spur. People seemed captivated by the energetic Coyote and his antics. We made many appearances together, encouraging people to take a look at the new Spurs with Larry Brown and a couple of young rookies from Arizona and Navy. Tim never seemed to wilt under the heat. He even appeared to gain strength as we went on, buoyed by the excitement of the fans. By the end of the summer, not being used to the Texas heat, I was exhausted. I could only imagine how much weight Mr. Coyote had lost while recruiting thousands of fans to the team.

It took a couple of years for the team to become more popular than the Coyote, but after some great successes, we began to get noticed. It didn't slow Tim down, though; he became more and more creative in his schemes and always kept the timeouts interesting. If it wasn't his high-flying dunk routines, it was his rappel from the roof or his unicycling balancing act that kept everyone watching. He was easily the most entertaining mascot in the NBA, along with the Gorilla of the Phoenix Suns. Over a period of time we met Mrs. Coyote and Coyote Jr., his son. After the Coyote had flirted with one too many female fans, we would often see Mrs. Coyote chasing him with a rolling pin. There was always something people could relate to.

The key to making any character come to life is believability. You must have the complete package and capture the imagination of the public. Tim definitely had that. No one ever thought about the guy behind the mask, because the Coyote had enough personality of his own. To this day, the thought of the Spurs without their beloved Coyote is something most Spurs fans could not fathom. He is an integral part of the San Antonio community. My sons have had several birthday parties highlighted by the furry guy. The Coyote pictures stand proudly beside Tim Duncan's and my own on the desk. It has been an unforgettable part of their childhood.

As I got to know Tim more in his personal life, I became deeply attached to the man. He holds many of the same values I so highly cherish, including love of family and dedication to his work. His family is wonderful, and I have only heard kind words and praise spoken of them. After Tim had his stroke, I got to see for myself their deep love for him. My wife, Valerie, and I visited with Colleen and Tim in the hospital and left encouraged by the overwhelming love we felt. All Tim seemed to be concerned with was taking care of his family and fulfilling his obligations as Mr. Coyote. He wanted to make sure the fans continued to get the same high-quality entertainment and love they had always gotten from their mascot. The show had to go on.

Tim ranks as one of the toughest men I have ever met. He couldn't walk, and even as he slurred his speech, he spoke of his inevitable recovery and asked what he could do for me. I told him to do the impossible for a character such as him—rest.

Now Tim works with the Spurs to ensure that the time outside the whistles on the court remains the most entertaining in basketball. With his beautiful wife and children, he continues to be one of the most blessed guys in the world.

David Robinson

Preface

What was the highlight of my career as an NBA mascot? The time I hung from a helicopter as it circled the airport over the heads of jubilant fans? When I caught a fastball thrown by Nolan Ryan? Or when I was hit in the face with a guitar by George Strait?

No, the most memorable of the 6,000 appearances I made as the Coyote occurred early one November. As I entered the neat suburban home, I got the picture right away, even with my vision partly obscured as it always was by the head of my costume. Christmas was more than six weeks away, but the tree was already decorated and blazing with lights, with wrapped presents heaped underneath. The boy I'd come to visit, no more than ten years old, was sitting up in a hospital bed in the living room. Beneath the shine of excitement over my visit, his face told its own tale: there were dark circles beneath his eyes, and the skin on his cheeks was papery white. I glanced over at his mother and father, who were watching the realization wash over me. Their boy was not long for this world.

I launched into my Coyote antics, clowning and joking. Laughter filled the room. And then I saw it. At the foot of the bed was a Super Mario Brothers game box. In those days, this was the Holy Grail for videogame fanatics, a fraternity in which I proudly claimed membership. Since becoming bedridden, the boy had developed into quite a talented player.

I picked up one of the controls; he picked up the other. The game was on. Joysticks became sticks of joy as we dueled and laughed for another hour and a half. Even encumbered by paws and a large head, I was a formidable foe. The contest ended when my opponent reluctantly surrendered to cheerful ex-haustion. I hugged him good-bye.

One week later, the boy's mother wrote to say that our game session was the first time in months her son had spontaneously smiled with glee. Seeing the

Coyote was exactly what he wanted for Christmas. He died three days after my visit.

They say laughter is the best medicine. Whenever I visited a hospital room, it was my goal to leave with heavy shoulders. I hoped to haul off the worries of the patients and their families, or at least to make them disappear for a moment or two.

On February 13, 2004, I was on such a mission in the intensive care unit of Brooke Army Medical Center. Wearing my furry suit, I entertained a young man and his mother by spinning a basketball on the tip of a fine-point pen.

Hours later I arrived at another hospital. But this time I was seeing the halls I knew so well from a stretcher.

I'd lost the ability to speak, to walk, and to move the right side of my body.

I could not return to the work I loved so dearly. The financial security of my family—a very real concern—was the least of my worries.

I was a stroke victim.

ONE
BEGINNINGS

Genius is one per cent inspiration,
ninety-nine per cent perspiration.

Thomas Alva Edison

People often ask me how I ended up as an NBA mascot. I've always thought of the path to my twenty-plus years as the Coyote as a string of happy accidents, a great big heap of serendipity. Lately, though, I see a pattern in the choices I made, in the opportunities I was offered. It's funny when you look back at the seemingly insignificant moments of your life. In hindsight you can see how they helped shape who you really are and made a big difference in where you ended up.

My mom once told me that my first words as a child were "Ta da!" That explains a lot. Most human bodies are 70 percent water. Mine was checked, and they found out I was 70 percent ham (smoked, I think).

Mom didn't show any surprise the day I was suspended from school in the fourth grade. She knew I would do just about anything to make people laugh. On this particular occasion I had taken off my shoes, in the middle of class, and thrown them out the window into the crisp snow below. My classmates did laugh. The teacher did, too, before she sent me to the principal.

I spent a lot of time in the principal's office in grade school. Little did I know, I was honing the skills that would later serve me well on the NBA hardwood: clowning in class, adroitly careening rubber bands onto the headdress of a nun's habit. What can I say? It was a gift.

Unfortunately, the head of the school didn't have a crystal ball. All she saw was a disturbance. I was a bit like Harry Potter, testing out the powers he doesn't quite have a handle on—and sometimes making a total mess of things. But as I grew older, things became clearer to me. I was destined to do something unusual. I wasn't sure what, but I knew it wouldn't be boring.

I've noticed that nobody who's successful works in a vacuum (unless his last name is Oreck!). We've all been influenced by those around us. Never does that become more obvious than when you think about your immediate family members.

My mom was a tomboy growing up. When she was a youngster in the 1930s, women weren't encouraged to participate in sports. There was no Mia Hamm to look up to. There were no Nike ads telling girls to "just do it." Gatorade was what you put on your skin if you got bitten by a crocodilian. Despite these road-blocks, my mom was an outstanding athlete: she played baseball with the boys, ran like the wind, and moved with grace. Her sister became a professional bowler.

Her brother is a real gem, too. When I was really young, I noticed a shiny medal on my uncle's Army uniform. Being a curious little guy, I asked him what it was. He said something about it being for marks-manship and changed the subject. Years later I learned that the medal he was modest about was the Distinguished Flying Cross. Success is no stranger to my mom's side of the family.

Dad was always downright funny. His physical condition has declined lately and he's lost much of his dexterity, but he's kept his humor and grace. Soon after he moved from Illinois to San Antonio to live in a retirement home near us, I noticed he had hung a plastic room service tag from his doorknob. The assisted care facility didn't deliver breakfast to the rooms; he knew that. He had swiped the tag from a swank hotel in Hawai'i years before and had been saving it for just such an occasion. The clown genes come from his side.

My brother, Jim, is a computer genius with General Electric. He is a Six Sigma Black Belt, which in layman's terms means he's a super genius. He is a great newspaper columnist, too: his article on the trials and tribulations of constructing the average American gas grill is classic. He also went to Hungary to adopt a small child. He came home with four, went back for one more, then added another. He now has seven adopted children under the age of thirteen.

My sister, Nancy Utley Jacobs, graduated with her

journalism degree and master's from Northwestern University. She's a recent widow and thus a single parent who, in her spare time, is the chief operating officer of Twentieth Century Fox Searchlight Pictures. She's considered by at least one source as the sixty-third most powerful woman in Hollywood (before J. K. Rowling and both Olsen Twins). Even knowing she lives in Lakers country doesn't sour my opinion that she's the smartest of the three of us.

With this family, I had no choice but to find some way to succeed in life. My poor dad! One child runs an arthouse motion picture studio. One child can research efficiency data and save millions of dollars for his company. And his middle child can . . . his middle child can . . . spin a basketball on a pen.

As a teenager living in a small, idyllic suburb of Chicago, I discovered the joys of tennis. In the beginning I wasn't very good, but I wanted to excel at it one day. Sadly, I picked up a bad habit—leading with my elbow when hitting a backhand. I learned a drill to correct my form, in which I put tennis ball A under my backhand armpit and then bounced tennis ball B, which I then hit. The idea was to hit ball B smoothly and not have ball A release until after the impact. If I led with my elbow, ball A would fall out first. Wrong! I must have bounced that ball a million times. I'd pound a tall, green backboard in my neighborhood until I got it right. I didn't have to set an alarm clock. No one came in to wake me up to practice. I was a kid on summer break. The early morning was cool and uncrowded, the perfect time to pulverize a yellow ball.

Some crazy people actually like to sleep in the morning. The neighbors who lived near the tennis courts were none too keen on the constant thumping. They begged my parents to keep their son indoors until the sun came up. I was a public nuisance, all because of my determination to become a good tennis player.

That determination did not waver. I had an important singles match while playing as a junior on the Glenbard West High School tennis team. My opponent and I might not have been exceptionally gifted, but we were evenly matched. I won the first set 11–9. I lost the second set 7–9. In the third and final set, we matched each other shot for shot. Neither of us wanted to lose; we were two motivated youngsters going head to head.

My home court advantage was significant: I was used to hearing the trains roar by on the tracks no more than twenty feet away. I timed my serves accordingly. He figured out what was going on and bent down to tie his shoe at strategic moments. We were both writhing in pain from cramps but unwilling to say uncle. Both of us had what looked like tennis balls under the skin of our calves where exertion had caused the muscles to knot. We were running on empty. I eventually won the last set 11–9. My worthy opponent had to be loaded directly into an ambulance. Exhibiting early signs of a lifelong aversion to ambulances, I was driven to the emergency room for an IV to relieve the painful cramps.

Partly because of that match, the high school athletics league instituted the tiebreaker. Officials wanted to avoid similar scenes in the future. This determination—some might call it stubbornness—proved fruitful, as I went on to be ranked number eight statewide for singles in Illinois.

Tennis brought me to San Antonio. I wanted to play for Trinity University, ranked number two in the nation. It's a long way from snowy, windy Chicago, but after thirty years here I can't imagine living anywhere else. The mosquito is the Texas state bird . . . but that's beside the point.

I recall my first visit to San Antonio, as a high school senior. I got off the plane, and there was a cute senior girl from the campus, ready to pick me up and give me a tour. Now at that time chasing the yellow ball was my first priority, but girls were a close second. "Are you Teee-eee-eeem?" she asked. Who knew my name had three distinct syllables! The southern accent was charming, and I knew in that instant I would marry a Texas girl someday.

I majored in business. Once, in an upper-level management class, our assignment was to describe the communication process in detail. The Big Mac had just come out and the new jingle was all over the place. With that in mind, I built a more interesting model of the communication process detailing the encode and decode process as buns, the sesame seeds as interference, and so on. My entire replica became a burger with two all-beef patties, special sauce, lettuce, cheese, pickles, onion, all on a sesame seed bun. I received an A. But in the right-hand corner of my report the professor had scribbled a note. It read, "What the devil are you doing in business?" He knew more about my future than I did.

After graduating from Trinity in 1979, I kept up my tennis game and paid the bills by working as a teaching tennis pro at the San Antonio Country Club. In the evenings, I kept my inner ham happy by appearing in musical productions with a community theater group and acting in melodrama productions (for which I was paid the princely sum of $10 for six performances a week).

After a few years of this, fate stepped into my life.

In 1983 I was appearing on stage in a Cole Porter music revue at the Trinity University Attic Theater. During one of my numbers, "Be a Clown," I dressed as a clown, walked on my hands while singing, hung from the ceiling. I was having a great time, chewing up the scenery. Unbeknownst to me, Jack Pitluck, head of a local public relations agency, had seen my performance. When Bob Bass, then general manager of the San Antonio Spurs, approached him sometime later with the idea of creating a mascot for the Spurs, Jack told him point-blank, "I don't know what we want for a mascot, but I do know who."

The next thing I knew, I was in the agency office being asked if I'd like to be an armadillo or a cowboy with a big mustache. Although I was flattered to be considered, I confessed that, being from Chicago, the only armadillo I had ever seen was belly-up on the side of the road. The cowboy theme belonged in Dallas. As an actor, I thought that creating a mascot character would be an artistic adventure. So I asked for a couple of weeks to think it over.

My dad and I had always loved Wile E. Coyote; to us, the stunts he tried were pure genius. And it didn't hurt that my brother-in-law was vice president of Warner Brothers at the time, giving me an easy avenue to check on trademark issues.

I pitched the Coyote character to all involved. *Entertainus carnivorous* was born. Jack Pitluck and Don Pausbach from the agency and Jim Goodman from the Spurs liked the idea. They each contributed their own creative suggestions. I thought of the Coyote as wily and quick, loving South Texas. A perfect fit for the Spurs.

I had to audition for Bob Bass in the gym at Trinity University. He laughed and shook his head when he saw me casually step to the free throw line and bang the basketball off my head. It caromed into the basket. He wasn't so amazed that I made the shot. He just loved the fact that someone would even think to attempt such a thing, let alone practice it. Truth is, after landing rubber bands on nuns' heads so many times before, this was easy. To this day, more than twenty years later, Bob still shakes his head and calls me "that damn Coyote" (without the last syllable *e*) in his heavy Oklahoma accent.

Another memorable occasion when the universe dropped a gift in my lap was after I'd been doing the Coyote for five years or so. There I was, quietly sitting in the HemisFair Arena bleachers, taking in the sights and sounds of the building before I was due to perform. This pregame sitting session had become a ritual for my assistant, Jon Fisher, and me. The Spurs staff was rehearsing a promotion on the court that required a contestant to spin a big disc, as on *Wheel of Fortune*, and then shoot from half-court. Bringing on the wheel, in classic Vanna White style, was this stunning young woman.

A tall, drop-dead gorgeous Texas girl. She oozed intelligence, charm, and grace. (As it turned out, she was working her way through college at the University of Texas at San Antonio and using this modeling job with the Spurs as a way to make ends meet while she got straight A's . . . although she has since admitted that she did indeed get one B—heaven forbid!)

I distinctly remember leaning over to Jon and saying quietly, "I don't know who that girl is, but I'm gonna marry her." Her name was Colleen Quirk. We ended up going out on a blind date set up by a friend, and two years later we were married. My mom's maiden name was Burke. So at the reception we had all the Burkes, Quirks, and Derks that Mission San José could handle.

I never wanted to be average. Nowadays, when I speak to a group of kids, I tell them that if you decide to smoke cigarettes, ditch school, and hang out behind the convenience store, it's your choice. You control your own actions. But then I tell them that if you pursue the things you love—whether it's playing Pokémon or poking a white ball in a small hole with a metal stick—and if you do the best you can, the rest of your life will follow. Those who settle for average will most likely end up there.

TWO
INNOCENCE AND WONDER

I simply put a piece of bologna under
each arm and I *feel* funny.

Steve Martin

I got the Coyote suit only two hours before my first
game. It was a rare double-header against the Los
Angeles Lakers in 1983. Along with all the other fans,
I paid to park at the arena. I walked into the game
hauling brown plastic trash bags filled with the Coyote
parts I would wear. If you ever saw a little blond guy
with brown trash bags walking by you in the early
days, that was me. Hefty was the unofficial luggage of
the San Antonio Spurs Coyote. For years I used an
imaginary fellow named Juan de la Basura (which

trips off the tongue better than John of the Garbage) in my introductions. Those bags were my inspiration.

The Coyote's uniform has a story all its own. Back in the day, no three-point line had yet been considered. When a player was fouled in the act of shooting, the referees would react dramatically and make a big downward arm motion to "count it!" if the foul shot went in. That was the drama I hoped to capture with the "2!" (I made the exclamation point a little askew so that from a distance the number wouldn't look like a "21.") The Coyote would jump up after a home basket and simply point to his jersey, as if to say, "Two, baby!"

I wasn't allowed in the pressroom in the early days. Today I joke to the mascots that my name was officially "Down in Front." This mascot thing was relatively new territory. There was no game plan. Everything we did was on the fly. We learned by trial and error. The Spurs did very few promotions at the time, so I was free to improvise during up to six timeouts a game. I'd see a roll of duct tape, a paperclip, and some blue paint in the corner of my dressing area, and I'd just make something out of it. I was MacGyver in fur.

There was no dressing room for Coyote at the beginning either. The opposing coaches would give their postgame press conferences right there in the room I used to change into and out of my gear. Pat Riley, then head coach of the Lakers, just plain hates mascots. He would calmly talk to the press while looking at me with real disgust as I took off my tail. I always felt as if he was thinking, "Why don't you get a real job—like mine?"

Later on I graduated to a dressing room that was nothing more than a glorified men's bathroom. Dignitaries would come in and relieve themselves, ignoring the little furry guy in the corner. It amazes me that my identity—who was that masked coyote?—remained a secret for more than twenty years.

The actor Charlie Sheen was a good friend of Spurs player Frank Brickowski. There was a period when he came to quite a few games. Shortly after *Platoon* was released, I improvised a parody, crawling like a Marine in my furry suit, with full camouflage gear and a water pistol. After filming *Major League*, in which he plays a pitcher nicknamed Wild Thing, Sheen attended a game and stopped by my stall-filled dressing room at halftime, wearing a Cleveland Indians hat from the movie shoot. Evidently oblivious to the fact that I was dripping sweat and was barely breathing from heat exhaustion, he said calmly, "You're really good. You want a cigarette?" I declined "butt" thanked him for the compliment.

It's funny to remember that smoking was allowed in the arena back then. All the clouds would eventually waft their way up to the balcony, making the arena look like nothing so much as a 16,000-seat bingo parlor.

Those were the days of Dr. J, the Iceman, and a young rookie by the name of Michael Jordan. Even now, I smile when I think of how kids would follow me all the way upstairs after being told by their parents to "be back by halftime." It was a safer time to be in sports.

It was during this era that a Miami Dolphin field goal kicker, Uwe von Schamann, botched a crucial field goal attempt. It made television news shows across the country. I parodied the event by kicking my own special toilet paper field goals into the crowd that night. Dressed in football gear, Coyote was Uwe von Charmin.

William "The Refrigerator" Perry was big back then, too. He played for the Chicago Bears and was famous for his appetite. He was massive. The Coyote came out in his own Bears uniform one evening. Picture the Michelin Man on steroids. I had half that morning's edition of the *San Antonio Express-News* and my favorite pillow from home tucked under my shirt. I ran toward the mini-trampoline to attempt dunking, as Refrigerator Perry, over a real refrigerator. The springs of the tramp snapped on impact since I had replaced them with skimpy rubber bands. When the tramp bed collapsed, I sat down nonchalantly and began eating. The obese Coyote reached over to the refrigerator, opened the door, and proceeded to stuff a loaf of bread and a pound cake into his mouth. Just like when I threw my shoes out the window in fourth grade, I was doing something because it felt funny to me. The crowd laughed.

In those early days the communication of cues and entrances had to be nonverbal since there was no way to speak to Coyote underneath all that fur. Then a newfangled gadget came on the market. You can see families at Disneyland today using Walkabouts, small battery-operated walkie-talkies, to keep track of each other. I bought a pair and stuck one up in my Coyote foam head. A Spurs employee had the other one. We debuted this new technology at an appearance at which Coyote would unveil a photograph for Spurs owner Peter Holt in front of a veritable sea of reporters. I needed to know exactly when to pull back the curtain, unveiling Coyote and his new portrait. The new communications system seemed perfect for the job. I hid behind that curtain for thirty-five minutes. None of the journalists had any idea I was back there. So far, so good. When it was just about time for me to receive my verbal cue, I heard two gentlemen conversing in my ear. "Do you want ketchup on your burger?" "Yeah, and if you can put a little mustard on there, too." Turns out that anyone using the same channel could be heard speaking. I was doomed. I had to switch back to "intuitive" timing. All was well, but only I knew how tricky it was to execute that precise timing. And not only that . . . I'd been waiting behind that curtain for a long time, and that burger they were talking about sounded good!

It's truly amazing how things just grew. In the beginning, there was no demand for the Coyote anywhere.

Barely anyone knew who he was. I'd tool around in my Volkswagen (a Coyote in a Rabbit). When I saw a group of people standing around, I'd pop out and start to clown. Half the appearances I made during my first few years were as an uninvited guest. In contrast, during his eighteenth year the Coyote made 444 public appearances and worked more than sixty games in three countries.

For one of my first appearances, I showed up on a scalding summer day at a local grocery store. The Spurs were giving an outside basketball clinic and I attended it in full fur. The parking lot was packed with fans. I tried my best to ignore the heat. After being there only a few minutes, I felt as if I were walking in quicksand. A child spoke up: "Excuse me, sir. You left part of your foot back there." He was correct. The rubber crepe on the bottom of the Coyote's big foot had melted onto the black pavement.

Speaking of malfunctioning feet, there was the time, early in my career, when I made a grandiose entrance on the second floor of a local mall. I was eager to make a dramatic impression, and the proud, cocky way I held out my arms as I entered proved it. Suddenly, as I was slowly rising on the escalator from the first floor on my way to the summit, my big Coyote foot got stuck in the steps. I was moments away from either breaking an ankle or being sucked into the basement. Unceremoniously, I yanked my foot out of the fur. Saved from near death perhaps, but I was dying from sheer embarrassment.

There are two kinds of timeouts in an NBA game. Regular timeouts are scripted. Unscripted "hot" time-outs come into play when the Spurs are on a tear and the opposing team calls for time. As an example: once the Spurs and Nuggets were tied 32–32 when the Spurs scored ten points in a row, punctuated with a slam dunk. I can still hear our public address announcer shouting as loud as he could, "Timeout Denver . . . how 'bout them Spurs!" That was Coyote's cue to take the floor.

Now this can be a pressure-filled situation, one that's hard on new mascots. I always saw hot time-outs as an opportunity to strut my stuff. It got so that I could smell them coming. I would feel the momentum building.

Russ Bookbinder, the Spurs' executive vice president for business operations (and a marketing genius) made it crystal clear early on. "Make an impact or get off!" he'd say. It was Russ who trained me to claim the center of the court. I reveled in the chance to be on center stage, freestyling for ninety seconds at a time.

Soon I began taking "audience participation" chances. Some worked, some didn't. "Go Spurs Go" was fail-safe from the beginning. I would lead two sides of the arena in alternating rounds of the cheer, encouraging a competition for the highest decibel level. Once I noticed the team's name painted on center court, just as I was beginning a hot timeout. I motioned the sound booth to cut the music, then jumped, with exaggerated staccato movements, on each letter while the fans yelled out the letters. "S-P-U-R-S—Spurs!" became a staple routine. For fun once I jumped on the letters backward. Hearing the crowd shout "S-R-U-P-S—Srups!" was hilarious. And, of course, Coyote's signature bit was directing fans in a memorable, united "Hey!" while "Rock 'n Roll Part II" blared over the sound system.

As the years progressed I began wearing an earpiece so that the press table could keep me informed of how much of a timeout remained. During tele- ·

vised games and during the play-offs, timeouts are much longer. I've had timeouts that lasted six minutes during the play-offs. In these extended performances, I would gradually stir the fans into a frenzy, carefully timing the crescendo of crowd noise. But every now and then, just as I was ready to launch into my blazing finish, I would hear "You've got two more minutes!" in my earpiece. Two more minutes? When I'd already been jumping around so wildly that I could scarcely breathe? Two more minutes? When I no longer had the strength to lift my arms above my head?

As a theater professional, I knew what I had to do. The show must go on.

I'd exit the court after an extended timeout and collapse on the floor backstage, unable to catch my breath. My assistant, Jon, had seen this dozens of times before. He knew from experience that I would find a breathing pattern. Usually I'd recover from my gasps, hop right up off the floor, and return to the court. While out-of-town NBC cameramen and EMT personnel new to the detail hovered over me, Jon could be seen casually drinking a soda off to the side, patiently waiting for me to breathe normally again.

He might hold my arms over my head to facilitate better breathing. But he remained calm and probably appeared unfeeling to any newbie watching. He cared, but he had seen it all before.

In the beginning, I had a minimum of six timeouts at every home game. I earned my keep, but I loved every minute of it. I used to drive home from games completely exhausted, sometimes in the grip of a hard-to-describe weepiness that comes from pure physical fatigue. During the 2003 play-offs, I didn't even bother to undress when I got home. I kicked off my shoes and walked down the steps into our pool. Submerged, I could feel the heat melt away; the cool water served as my jumbo-sized personal ice pack. That would have made a Lipton Iced Tea commercial to beat all others.

Unlike hot timeouts, regular timeouts are planned, scripted, and usually rehearsed. My skit was always during the second timeout of the first quarter. The idea was to do the skit before the game had heated up but late enough that the fans had found their seats.

In hindsight, November 18, 1995, is a memorable

night, but at the time it was a typical home game. The arena was packed with Spurs fans. I was eager to unveil a new movie parody. I made my way into the bowels of the referees' dressing room, where I met and talked with a gentleman who would become one of my dearest NBA friends. After hearing the premise of the skit, Dick Bavetta said, "Sure, I'd love it. Anything for you, Timmer."

I was in like Flynn.

After coming down from Cloud Nine, I explained that I would be dressed in full boxing regalia. While dancing to the theme from the new blockbuster *Rocky*, I would repeatedly taunt the ref and thrust my chin forward, daring him to give me his best shot. Being a ref, he would stoically ignore my antics until such time as he slyly reached behind his back. My assistant would place an unpadded rubber boxing glove on Dick's right hand. One comedic, well-placed roundhouse from the referee would complete the skit. The punch would hit the soft foam of the Coyote's cheeks, leaving me unhurt and the referee confident that everyone knew who was boss. A good time would be had by all. K-I-S-S—Keep It Safe and Simple—was my motto, and I left no stone unturned in my explanation of how the skit should go. Or so I thought.

Dick did as instructed, but his jovial right cross somehow became a hard right jab and landed squarely in the Coyote's mouth, very nearly the only vulnerable area he could reach. With a crunching sound, the Coyote's head snapped to the right and I went flying. Dick broke my nose and his finger at the same time. The crowd loved it and marveled at how realistic the punch looked. Of course they did!

I staggered to my feet and finished the skit in my woozy state, acting as if nothing out of the ordinary had occurred. Jon came out as if to help me, saying, "I'll get the trainer," under his breath. He knew I was hurt. I hustled to the dressing room. The trainer came in time to see me on my hands and knees over a good-sized puddle of blood, nose dripping. I stuffed tissue in my nostrils and wrapped my head with athletic tape, and I was ready for the next timeout.

After that, whenever Dick Bavetta went to the scorer's table to announce a foul, the press crew would cower and hide from him in jest. "Boom Boom" Bavetta was born that night. And I now know that I took a punch that would make my boxing friend James Leija, the Texas Tornado, proud. The legend has grown over the years. I frequently hear the story told, particularly by rookie mascots, as "some ref got so mad that he knocked out the Coyote." For the record, I was up before a ten count—but barely. If you look at my unmasked face closely, you'll see that my nose curves to the right. Now you know why.

Another skit for the ages involved Tanya Crevier, who had played in the old professional Women's Basketball League. On one occasion years ago, I learned that Tanya was going to perform her ball-handling exhibition for our halftime show. She graciously consented to appear in my skit during the first quarter. I had her dressed in civilian clothes, designed to hide her athleticism as much as possible, and then I planted her in the front row. No one knew who she was. With "Dueling Banjos" playing over the loudspeakers, I began to perform outrageous ball-handling tricks, for all the world looking as if I was showing off for the pretty girl in the front row. Tanya immediately began mirroring my every move, to the crowd's delight. When I responded with some "Well, you think you're so hot! Let's see what you can do" body language, off she went. She brought the house down with two-ball dribbling between her legs and ended with a chest pass directly into my furry face, knocking me down just as the music ended. Poor Coyote had gotten the short end of the chauvinistic stick.

While filming an episode of the *Coyote Clubhouse* TV program, I made a comic show of falling off a little horse. Less comically, for me anyway, I exploded the bursa on the elbow of my arm. I finished the appearance and noticed that my elbow had swelled to the size of a cantaloupe. Could one joint actually retain that much fluid? The only time I ever wore an additional elbow pad outside the fur suit was to protect this injury.

Two days later, the Mascot Slam Dunk championships took place, a live national telecast on NBC. The event was in San Antonio, with the Coyote as host. Squatch from the Seattle Supersonics chased an errant pass from the Charlotte Hornet and pulled off an amazing one-handed, arm-extended dunk. Next, Rocky from the Denver Nuggets went between the legs, to the delighted squeals of thousands of kids. The pressure was on. The Coyote was last, with 36,000 San Antonio children cheering him on. You know how athletes are supposed to visualize themselves succeeding? Well, all I could imagine was the groans of disappointed hometown school kids. But I had a fail-safe gimmick: a blindfolded dunk. The blindfold covered Coyote's eyes, but I looked out through the mouth of the costume. Often the best tricks are pure illusion. As I ran toward the tramp "blindfolded," I felt the squish of the fluid in my elbow. I made the dunk and won the competition. But it's one elbow injury I'd like to forget.

Alas, I'm finding it hard to do so. Near the Spurs office at the AT&T Center, where I go to work, hangs a life-sized photo of the Coyote wearing a black elbow pad—taken during the contest. I cringe every time I walk by that poster.

The bursa injury isn't the only one that makes me squirm when I think of it. Another time I tore my rotator cuff. Well, I tore both cuffs, but the right one was the more memorable. Dr. Bud Curtis was my man, the best shoulder guy in town, the Top Gun of shoulder surgeons. He knew my line of work and kept it close to the vest. One afternoon I went to his office because of constant shoulder pain. He entered the examination room with the X-ray he had just taken and began talking about my arm. I assured him that my arm felt fine and that I was there for my shoulder. He pointed out on the X-ray that I must have broken the arm at some point and gutted it out as a sprain. We both laughed. He knew I was different when it came to pain.

My rotator cuff was completely torn away from the bone. I explained that when dunking, to cushion my fall, I put out my right arm just as I hit the mat. This was what had caused the injury.

"How long have you felt pain?" he asked.

"About two years," I said.

"Two years? How many times have you put your arm out to cushion your fall?"

I told him that, counting rehearsals, I had probably dunked 2,000 times in this fashion. He just shook his head and scheduled the surgery. Since that day—and I have the videotape to prove it—I have dunked without putting out my right arm. Mama didn't raise no dummy.

I did my best to hide from the Spurs what I had to do to keep myself up and running. I scheduled all my surgeries during the off-season so the office personnel wouldn't know the half of it. I preferred it that way. One Spurs employee did catch me in the men's room once while I was urinating blood (one of the signs of a bruised kidney). He threatened to turn me in if I didn't see a doctor.

I also struggled for two years or more with plantar fasciitis, an affliction you wouldn't wish on your worst enemy, though many an athlete knows it well. Imagine a bruise from a sharp pebble right in the middle of your heal that continues and expands. They didn't show, but I'd wear padded heels under my Coyote feet in order to lessen the pain. It was worst in the mornings. I learned to crawl on my hands and knees to the bathroom before literally crawling back to bed. It became quite funny when my kids would nonchalantly say "good morning" as they saw their daddy go by on all fours on his way to use the potty or brush his teeth.

During my years as the Coyote I endured a broken nose, an exploded bursa, a torn meniscus, a completely torn hamstring, a cracked rib (twice), two torn rotator cuffs (left one fixed arthroscopically, the right using a scalpel), a boutonniere deformity on the pinkie finger of my dunking hand, a bruised kidney (twice), a rare case of pneumonia—the list goes on and on.

As Coyote, I had gotten into the habit of hanging over the railing of the upper level of the arena. But I broke that habit cold turkey when I was hamming it up one night. While leaning out somewhat precariously, I realized that the railing I was hanging onto was removable. It simply came away in my hand, leaving me no anchor at all to hold on to. I was forced to jump some twenty feet below, metal gate in hand, to concrete. Thank goodness I hit no one. But the impact on the bottom of my feet was excruciating. I couldn't even limp because I hurt both feet; I had to crawl a lot that night on the court. No one seemed to notice.

No matter what the ailment or domestic problem, the show had to go on.

When I was fresh out of college I bought a darling little pooch. She cost $7.56 but was priceless to me. I called her Taxi, and we were inseparable. I heard a comedian say that he once lost his dog Taxi in New York, and I thought it was funny (think about it for a while). It must have been amusing to hear me shout

"Taxi! Taxi!" when I wanted her to come inside. She ran with me. She shopped with me. Even untethered, she never left the yard. She sat on the table when I ate and never begged. She rode in the car with me. She had class and grace.

She was so cute (like Benji, only better) that I soon learned of her powers as a chick magnet. She helped me reel in a single goddess named Colleen. Seventeen years passed and Taxi had grown to love my wife, too. Taxi and I were like Laurel and Hardy or the average American and credit card debt—a match made in heaven. When she grew older and was nearing the end of good health, I just prayed that she would last a little longer. She was nearly blind and definitely deaf, and I felt for her.

Then it happened.

In the dark, I backed the car out of my driveway to head to the Alamodome and felt a thump. I assumed I had hit a neighbor's bike or a cardboard box. It was Taxi. Somehow the dog had escaped my watchful eye and crept out of the house. She couldn't see or hear my car, and I couldn't see her in the dark. I wept as if I'd lost a close relative. Only minutes from tip-off, I had to bury my best buddy in the side yard and then head to work. The Coyote had a great evening, no doubt. But I was miserable.

The show must go on.

The limited view from the Coyote suit made it difficult to do a lot of physical feats. Even dunking, which I did hundreds of times, was not as simple as it looked to the fans. Neither the rim of the basketball hoop nor the tramp itself, for that matter, were visible to me inside that big furry head. "Coyote vision" didn't include anything remotely peripheral. In fact, the costume didn't even allow me to look straight ahead. Every time I did a dunk, I had to take it on faith that the tramp was positioned correctly. As I ran up, carefully counting out the predetermined number of steps, all I saw was wood, wood, wood until at last I'd see the tramp and then a second later the orange rim.

At the same time, I loved the way the costume allowed me the freedom to hide my "human" ailments. I liked to give the impression that I was having fun even when I had one eye closed and the other stinging from sweat. The salt pain only made it that much more challenging and thus rewarding. I loved it.

Not all the Coyote moments were hardships. In my bachelor years, my assistant would kid with me by having single women talk into his microphone when I couldn't see him. His microphone, of course, fed into my earpiece. I'd hear these sultry female voices in my ear at random times during the game. I have been asked to autograph all sorts of body parts. While I was signing one sinuous thigh during a game, an imaginary red flag went up, telling me to stop. I realized that this beautiful young woman was most likely drunk, and it wasn't a good idea to take her at her word when she implored me to "sign higher."

Every night for many years, Jon "Radar O'Reilly" Fisher and I would throw Frisbees to the crowd. The fans knew that coupons for free pizza were attached to the bottoms of these plastic discs. A Mark McGwire home-run ball couldn't create a frenzy to compete with the one caused by our little Frisbees and their orange coupons. Eventually I tired of the normal routine of catching under the leg and began experimenting with different toss techniques. I wanted to try something new. One night I boldly told Jon that during our next timeout I'd like to make a long-distance basket with the Frisbee. He just laughed at the notion but knew I'd at least try my darnedest.

I stood behind the opposite free throw line. My first attempt was a little short but taught me the range. My second toss arched gracefully to the left and then banked hard to the right as planned. "Swish" was all I heard as the disc went through the net without hitting the rim. I raised my arms in triumph, not caring if the fans appreciated or even noticed what had just happened. This trick was for me. No half-court backward shot had ever come close to the exhilaration I felt that night. For a single moment I was the Tiger Woods of Frisbee Golf. I'm still waiting for a call from Nike about a lucrative contract. I guess they misplaced my number.

In the early years, Coyote was a freelancer—performing at Spurs home games and making promotional appearances as requested by the organization. I supplemented my income, and perfected the Coyote character, by making appearances at venues throughout the country.

At one time, the Continental Basketball Association was a kind of minor league for the NBA—a league with a much diminished budget. Once I asked to borrow two towels for my performance. I watched in amazement as the team equipment manager made me two towels by ripping one in half.

At some point in the early 1990s, a very funny but less-than-reputable promoter, who shall remain nameless, failed to pay me. He also refused to pay the Bud Light Daredevils; a chain-saw juggler; and the featured celebrity, a boxer who was the World Welterweight Champion at the time. When this promoter gave me empty promises about future payment, I felt there was nothing I could do. The boxer was determined not to leave without his money, however. Five rather large gentlemen took the tightwad promoter into a room, where they discussed their desire for prompt payment. As you might expect, the pugilist and his entourage exited the room with money in hand, followed by one pale, sweaty promoter. I was 148 pounds soaking wet. I had to use brains instead of brawn.

After three years of fruitlessly hounding the promoter by phone, I hatched a plan. Soon after Al Gore invented the entire Internet, I used a popular search engine to find the investor whose money had been behind the event. I reached him directly the first time I phoned. He listened intently while I explained that he and I were cool, but he might like to know that his event promoter was shafting people left and right. We talked about our families and otherwise had a great catch-up conversation. After we got off the phone, it wasn't ten minutes before I received a call from you-know-who. I might have been only a piece of cheese to this sleazy promoter, but he was a mouse who definitely wanted to keep the cat happy, and I knew it. He rudely demanded that I meet him in the food court of the local mall. I considered leaving a note for my wife in case anything happened, but we met and talked without incident. Then he reached under the table and pulled the long-overdue cash from his cowboy boot. I thought it was a strange way to be paid, but I wasn't going to ask any questions. Makes me want to name my next dog Google.

At one Wichita Falls Texans game, the promoters shrewdly handed out 6,000 rubber mini-basketballs to the fans in attendance. I was the featured entertainer, and things were going along swimmingly—in fact, the makeshift basketball court was set atop a filled pool. Suddenly, the referee called a bad foul on the home team. Soon afterward came a second bad call. Boos rained down from the stands.

My trusty assistant yelled at me, "Get off the court now!" I didn't know exactly what was happening, as was often the case due to my limited vision in the Coyote head, but I knew Jon well enough not to question his judgment. I exited pronto. Seconds later, all 6,000 of the giveaways were being hurled onto the court in the direction of the referee. "Mini-ball night" had become "projectile night." I'll forever remember the sound of all those bouncing rubber balls. Nowadays at the AT&T Center we sell soft drinks in plastic bottles sans caps to avoid anyone getting injured in a similar situation.

I would often squeeze in out-of-town gigs while the Spurs were on the road. Once I performed for the Quad City Thunder up in snowy Moline, Illinois, in the dead of winter. I asked the game operations manager where their catwalk was because I needed to tie off my 100-foot rope in order to rappel into the arena for my big entrance. He just pointed toward the roof. No indoor catwalk existed. I figured I didn't fly all this way to be boring. So I stuck to my plan, which meant that I had to go out in the cold, climb onto the roof of a car, jump onto the roof like Santa, release an old rusted hatch, and then rappel down when I heard my name being announced. All this in costume, mind you! Entering the warm building in costume during the first timeout, I laughed as I looked down at the hardwood far below and saw my still snow-covered Coyote feet leading the way.

My mom drove in from my childhood home, three hours away, to see this performance. What thanks did she get? I stole her fur coat and dramatically mimed mouth-to-mouth resuscitation and CPR on the poor beast.

These days we never send out the Coyote, or any of our mascots, without an assistant. It's always helpful to have another set of working eyes and a good set of opposable thumbs around. In the early years I wasn't so lucky. No cell phones existed, but I knew which pay phones were situated just right so that I could reach out to dial with my furry arm and go unnoticed by passersby. If I only had a nickel for each time I spent 35 cents calling for directions and driving in full costume. My secret identity would have been in peril with one wreck. Later on I had that big black brick of a cell phone with the antenna. I thought I was cool when I called my wife and said, "Hi, honey, I'm calling you . . . from the car." And today we've graduated to GPS computer systems. Ah, progress!

The best illustration of why I needed an assistant wasn't the day I was nearly hit by a car while in the middle of a downtown street. (I managed to dodge that one, though barely.) This time I was sent to the Bright Shawl, an upscale San Antonio party house, to perform at a Christmas event. I had been instructed to pull out all the stops and give my best effort. I arrived complete with Santa costume ("Santa Claws," I called it) and a bag full of gifts I had scrounged from the Promotions Department. I was loaded for entertainment pleasure. This venue had two party rooms. I entered the building not knowing which room to enter. I heard "Coyote! We're so glad you could make it!" coming from one side. I followed that voice, greeted everyone in attendance, did all the physical comedy I could think of, posed for pictures, and handed out the gifts I had brought.

After nearly an hour and a half, I left the party exhausted but with the distinct feeling of a job well done. As I was exiting, I saw a woman directly across the hall with her hands on her hips. "Well, there you are!" she said. "You're late." I had gone to the wrong Christmas party! I was not only blind in that costume; I was stupid. I had no gifts and no energy, but I made the most of the party's remaining time by mingling in my best holiday spirit. No wonder those other revelers had been so nice.

Some of my wildest Coyote adventures took place in Europe. I was in Spain once for a multigame basketball tournament. One night, after the fans and I had gotten to know each other, I found my small frame being hoisted up and passed around the stadium. I just kept my body stiff in order to avoid hitting what I later labeled "fan turbulence." There was a definite soccer atmosphere to the crowd. They were singing, in Spanish of course, some local song as they passed me down the aisles. I couldn't understand what they were singing, but they sounded happy and totally complimentary. Later I asked my interpreter about it. He explained that they were chanting a traditional Spanish song proclaiming that they loved the Coyote. They proudly declared that I had "the biggest *cojones* in all of Spain" and they wished me good health. He said it was high praise indeed. I'd hate to hear what they'd sing if they didn't like you!

At an appearance in France, I listened to the foreign P.A. announcer launch into his introduction. Perched high atop a six-foot unicycle, I suddenly realized that despite all my meticulous preparations—finding the mats, running through the routines to make sure I had the distances down pat, testing my equipment—I had no idea what he was saying or when to enter. I just stayed put until I heard what I prayed was the word *Coyote* (just imagine Inspector Clouseau saying it), and off I rode.

In a parking lot performance in Mexico City, the organizers wanted us to dunk with only a six-foot area to run—insufficient for me or my dunking cohort. The stage was elevated about six feet so that the crowd could see. I figured that I hadn't come all that way to give up. I had them park a Suburban and an ambulance lengthwise, against the stage, so I could get a longer run at the basket. I still chuckle when I think of myself, in costume, leaping from vehicle to vehicle and then onto the stage. I imagine it's the closest I'll get to being Harrison Ford in the movies.

On my second trip to Mexico as Coyote, I did a series of performances in various cities. On the flight from Guadalajara to Chihuahua, I heard what sounded like roosters crowing in the luggage compartment beneath my seat. I thought nothing of it—after all, the sun was indeed rising that early morning as we landed. It was 104 degrees in the shade (now I know why Chihuahuas are a toasted brown color).

A throng of people filled the runway. Armed guards stood at attention, and Mexican police lights flashed.

All this for me? I thought. I must have been really good in Guadalajara.

Suddenly the pilot's voice came over the intercom and instructed us to stay on the plane while our "celebrities" were unloaded. I slicked back my hair a little, preparing to meet the reporters. I blushed with modesty and rose from my seat. The stewardess politely asked me to remain seated.

A dozen brightly colored roosters were gently un-packed from the bottom of the plane. The crowd, followed by the armed guards, departed with the birds, leaving me baking in the aluminum fuselage that had become my temporary cage.

I later learned that the birds were a cherished breed of fighting cock. They were traveling the country, and everywhere they went, they were treated like rock stars.

When I was finally allowed to deplane, I had a good laugh. Not a soul was there to meet me. I was just a varmint with nowhere to go. The phrase "from hero to goat"—or was it "from hero to Coyote"?—was nearly true.

I swear I knocked 'em dead in Guadalajara the night before.

Ask my kids what has four wheels and an engine, and they'll say a car. Ask them what you park in a garage, and they'll say, "Two smelly heads, four suits, and a bunch of really neat props." They've never seen a car parked in our garage. I've always needed the space for my Coyote work. When I had writer's block, I'd go into the garage and look at everything I had on the shelves and wait for comedic inspiration. It worked most days.

THREE
GLORY DAYS

Creativity makes a leap, then looks to
see where it is.

Mason Cooley

One of the most creatively satisfying parts of my job
was video making. In flagrant imitation of David
Letterman, I'd start the bit live at the beginning of a
timeout, and then on some flimsy pretext—"Oh, I
need to go get something"—I'd leave the floor. We'd
switch to the monitors with a video of Coyote having some comic adventure before I'd show up again
on the floor, to finish the skit off in real time.

Back in 2000, after the Spurs won the NBA title for
the first time, I had access to the new NBA trophy. I
wasn't going to pass up the opportunity to work with

that sleek reflective sculpture as a prop in one of my video skits. I had long yearned to have a mock group of NBA mascots playing poker together in a dingy room. Now I just had to work the trophy into the skit.

A ceiling fan cast great shadows on a green felt table. All the mascots were phony, but they looked real in the video. The Phoenix Gorilla bet with a bunch of yellow bananas. The Charlotte Hornet was all in with a big jar of honey. The Chicago Bull folded. The Milwaukee Buck wagered a forty-pound bag of dog food marked "Purina Buck Chow." And then it was the Vancouver Grizzly's turn.

I had approached the fish counter of the H-E-B grocery in search of what I wanted the Grizzly to put up: a big salmon of some kind. I was completely taken aback when the guy behind the counter (What do you call a "fish butcher" anyway . . . Gill?) asked, "You want that fish with eyes or without?" I had no idea I'd have a choice. Of course, I asked for the fish with eyes. Without moving his feet, without any hesitation, he knelt briefly behind the counter and rose with the most beautiful thirty-eight-pound Pacific salmon I had ever seen. Still with its head on. Looking as if it had been caught maybe ten minutes earlier. For a moment I pictured David Copperfield under that counter, conjuring up exotic items to make customers happy.

So the Grizzly unceremoniously plunked the salmon down on the table, and all heads turned to the Coyote. I glanced into the eyes of my card-playing opponents and then jubilantly trumped them all by producing the NBA championship trophy. I had five aces of Spurs in my hand, too. I won the hand as they all retreated, in awe of the trophy. I had a good laugh, too, picturing our accounting department collectively shaking their heads over the $84 expense receipt for a fish.

Early in my career I learned that if things could go wrong, they often would.

Years ago I came up with the clever idea of dressing the Coyote like a Christmas tree. I could picture it clearly. The mascot would be stuck with his long ears popping out and that big nose protruding from the disguise. I announced to the crowd that there would be no Coyote that evening due to inclement weather at the Dallas–Fort Worth airport. The crowd moaned and voiced its disapproval just as I had hoped it would. Our P.A. announcer then offered a consolation, asking the fans to reach under their seats for "the official Spurs song sheet" and to join in singing "Rockin' Around the Christmas Tree." My favorite part of this bit was hearing all the seats being lifted as a good majority of the fans searched for that fictitious song sheet.

Then the Coyote entered in his holiday disguise. Dressed completely as a tree, with ornaments and lights attached, he tiptoed onto the court and used a Polaroid camera to slyly take a photo of the opposing team's huddle. He waited for the image to develop and promptly carried the picture to the head coach on the Spurs bench. It seemed foolproof.

One evening near Christmas, during a game against the Washington Bullets, I ran into a little snag. Manute Bol, whose 7'7" height made him an imposing defensive presence on the court, had an impressive wingspan. Before I could hand over the photo to our coach, Bol's condorlike arms swooped down to snatch the picture from the camera, leaving me with nothing. With my punch line stolen, I improvised a new finish, making a big show of moving farther away to snap a new picture. After that night,

I revised the skit so that I used a clipboard and marker instead of a camera. Monitor and adjust!

I'm often asked about the exact origin of my "Dancing on the Ceiling" routine in HemisFair Arena, in which I would hang from a rope, then put my furry feet on the ceiling of the balcony to dance upside down. The answer is somewhat embarrassing. By the mid-1980s rappelling from the balcony had become the norm for Coyote. But on one game night I hadn't properly tightened the "seat"—the leather straps that were cinched tightly around my midsection to attach me to the rope. I was tethered safely but not tightly enough. Mid-rappel, I felt the harness I was wearing slip to my knees. I knew that as long as I kept my legs bent, it was safe. I figured that if trapeze artists could hang on, so could I. As fate would have it, this hanging action left me upside down on the rope looking directly at the ceiling. My assistant, Jon, was yelling "Great idea!" and giving me the thumbs-up, never for a moment thinking I might be in peril. I simply put my feet on the ceiling, grabbed the rope extra tight, and danced as if it were all planned. Add a Lionel Richie hit and you've got a skit!

In another memorable skit that didn't go off exactly as planned, I was hooked up to some pretty powerful pyrotechnics. I had dressed cautiously, but when I reached down to adjust the zipper on one foot, I accidentally activated the trigger mechanism for the explosive powder. Sparks thirty feet high flew off my ankles. I quickly sat on the floor under the stands, aiming the flames away from those around me. It gave new meaning to the expression "hot timeout."

I have had two assistants who deserve membership in the mythical "assistant hall of fame" for their efforts.

Jon Fisher pledged Chi Delta Tau fraternity, where I was a member, when he was a sophomore and I was a junior at Trinity. I was in the frat for sports; I didn't drink or party much. That's one thing Jon and I had in common. We also had a sense of humor that other people thought was a little off and a tendency to think outside the box. We got along splendidly.

The physical endurance tests required of pledges were a piece of cake for Jon. But the drinking challenges? Another story. He needed a guardian angel.

So I took him under my wing and made sure he was never required to do anything he didn't want to do. I was by no means bucking my responsibilities as an active in the fraternity. Pledges had to earn their induction. On more than one dark and rainy night, I was out on the football field with the other actives, mercilessly hectoring the pledges, Jon included. But all the while, I'd manage to serve him water instead of beer or maybe pour out his drink while the other actives weren't looking. (Of course, I did make him do my laundry in exchange for the protection.)

Over the years our friendship grew, reinforced by the different paths we followed. Jon worked a succession of "normal" jobs in retail and then insurance while I went the starving actor route. Let's put it this way: he had health insurance *waaay* before I did. We lived through each other's lives a bit. I toyed with the idea of going legit (read nine to five); he wondered what it would be like to throw care to the wind and just perform.

Jon was my best man. True to form, he not only served the groom, he took care of the three groomsmen as well, serving three flavors of Gatorade before the hot August wedding. When I began thinking about the Coyote gig, there was no question about who should assist me. We effortlessly fell back on our old college hobbies—Frisbee golf, intramural sports, and of course obscure humor—for our on-court shenanigans.

One of Jon's most memorable "Johnny on the spot" performances was when he noticed that I was wearing the wrong color leotard as I prepared to parody a strength act that had just performed at halftime. I was buffed out in a beige muscle-bound suit preparing to imitate the Alexis Brothers, who were famous for their strength moves (some of them actually illegal in Minnesota, I think). The gentlemen performers were dressed in blue, and I desperately wanted to match them. I hurriedly shouted to Jon that there must be a can of blue spray paint somewhere in the building. I would dress in the beige and let him spray me from shoulder to foot in blue paint. He disappeared, and three long minutes passed while I fretted about having to go on to the court shortly. Then I saw Jon sprinting down the hall with an aerosol can in his hand. I held my breath as he sprayed the paint. (The fumes were disgusting.) Just as we finished, the scoreboard horn sounded. The time was now. I entered the court not knowing whether the paint was even dry. I guess I was the original Blue Man Crew!

The second hall of famer is Greg Piehl. I was asked to entertain some Spurs fans at the airport as they patiently waited for the team to return home after winning our first championship. I left twenty minutes before the flight was due to arrive, as I had done countless times before. This time we were caught in a tremendous traffic jam. Much to my surprise, thousands of people lined the airport and tarmac to show their support for the team. Greg quickly jumped out of the car and approached a policeman. Within minutes we were in a police escort, bypassing traffic even if it meant we had to drive on the sidewalk at times. We never would have made it to the terminal without his quick thinking. But there's more to the story. Once there, I began entertaining the throng. A few minutes later I realized it was 110 degrees on the cement and that I needed help. I couldn't last at this rate. I gave Greg a big hug, as if I was excited to see him (that's our signal for "I have something to ask you"), and made a plea to my human helper.

Without mincing words, I muttered, "I need a helicopter!" I knew it probably wasn't feasible, but I wanted to buzz high above the crowd and generate more excitement. I half-expected him to quit right then and there. But he didn't bat an eye and began examining the nearby hangars. Then, like Lassie disappearing on a mission, he was gone. Only six minutes passed before he returned, out of breath, and said, "Follow me!" We ran about 500 yards, and there was a TV helicopter with its rotors already churning, waiting for my arrival.

We flew over the crowd and had an incredible time. I asked the pilot if I could lean out of the cockpit, thinking there might be some obscure FAA rule or something (heck, they tell you not to put your arms out on the kiddie train at our local zoo). "I don't care what you do," he said. "Just don't let go, is all I ask." What a dream mascot moment! The Coyote was a hit, my antics were all over the news, I took all the glory, and Greg was really the one who deserved it.

Good assistants are more valuable, by the pound, than gold.

At a home game a few years ago, I became aware of a huge gathering of Lackland Air Force Base recruits in one section of the arena. I knew this was perhaps the only night these brave men and women had, during their six weeks of basic training, to let off a little steam. I felt for them.

I made one pantomime motion while I was on the court. Jon was on the case. From clear across the court, without a single word from me, he knew what was on my mind. When I came off the hardwood a few minutes later he already had a soldier willing to disrobe and give his unmistakable blue shirt and tie to a mangy stranger, as long as we promised to hide him from his superiors. We showed him a secret spot under the stands where he could watch the stunt unfold. I put on my Spurs warm-up top and ran up to the section to welcome the soldiers. They cheered and I grunted and we had loads of fun. But when I stripped off my jersey and revealed my Air Force uniform, I was immediately one of the gang to them. We high-fived, danced, waved our fists, and got tons of TV airtime. I returned the shirt after I got back to my "den," and the generous recruit returned to his seat as if he'd been in the bathroom and missed it all. You couldn't have pulled off a jewel heist with more precision.

I had designed the costume to have removable eyes. Sometimes I would substitute eyes that showed extreme emotions, like horror or surprise. Other times I'd simply rip out the eyes and offer them to the ref after an offensive foul was called. One night I took off the eyes and coyly slid them over to veteran referee Tommy Nuñez. He casually observed me taunting him and waited. He knew my character had to be sightless while my eyes were off. He bent down, picked up the eyes, and instead of showing them to the crowd as he normally would, he simply put them down the front of his pants. He walked away getting the last laugh that day.

Always wanting to try something fresh and new, I came up with the idea that the Coyote would ascend to the top floor of the AT&T Center and heave a football all the way down to the court. I even wore brown garden gloves that hid my identity but provided the necessary dexterity for throwing. I practiced for two days, precisely measuring the throw. Soon I could hit the target every time. I assured the Spurs brass that every base had been covered.

The night of the big game arrived. We cued up the video showing all the trials and tribulations I had to go through on my way to the top floor. Everything was going smoothly. I suddenly appeared live on the upper level and noticed two referees standing with their backs to me, almost exactly on the spot I'd been using as my target. Surely they'll move, I thought. Besides, what were the odds that I'd hit anybody from way up here?

I waited and then heaved the ball to my assistant below. The ball arced as if in slow motion (I can still picture it), gathering speed as it headed for its mark. Needless to say, I missed my assistant and hit one of the referees squarely in the back of the head. (He was built like a house, too.) The crowd cheered with glee, and of course I acted as if I'd done it on purpose. But any shrewd fan could see me at the next timeout, standing next to the rather stout gentleman in the striped shirt. To remain in character, I kept looking straight ahead, which meant I had to scream in order for my profuse apologies to be heard.

Sometimes I would do things that only one small pocket of fans could see. One time I was near Spurs owner Peter Holt when I saw a crack in the court that was out of bounds but nonetheless quite noticeable. The court was hollow, so I knew anything dropped in that crack would fall harmlessly to the cement floor below. Throughout the game that night, I would get Peter's attention and slide dollar bills and loose change I had into the slot. I knew he was wondering what I could possibly be doing. His whole section became more curious each time I deposited money in the wooden slot. It wasn't until the fourth quarter that I showed up with a piece of duct tape marked "Coyote's 401K" and stuck it next to the crack. Just a few people saw it, but they definitely got a chuckle out of it. Impromptu moments like that were loads more fun for me than the scripted ones.

Speaking of impromptu, I was home nursing a torn hamstring one winter day when the UPS guy came to my door delivering a small box that contained some Christmas gifts. I opened the box and then spent the next twenty minutes cleaning up all the foam peanuts that were inside. I looked over to see my son, who was four at the time, playing in the box. A sign from heaven.

In my best little-kid English, I asked Griffin if he thought he could curl up and hide in that little box. He did. I explained that many kids could hide, but only those really special children could learn to be shut in the box and jostled like a real package. We practiced, and by the time my wife came home I was carrying the box around the house with Griffin curled up inside, laughing. We did this three times a day for a week.

The next home game was just before Christmas. I had the Coyote, dressed up as Santa, doling out gifts to various "random" individuals. After emptying my satchel of goodies, I walked by the officials, acting sorry that I had not gotten them anything. But then I acted out getting a bright idea and produced this rather small box from beneath the basket. I shook the box a little, just like in the rehearsals at home.

I deposited my package in front of the referees and exited to the corner of the court to watch. The ref opened the lid and my young son stood up, wearing a complete elf outfit with leggings. (Note to my son: You'll no doubt be seeing pictures of this at your rehearsal dinner someday.) He gave one official a great big Christmas hug and a candy cane. Then he stomped on the other ref's foot and ran to me. The Coyote had three dollars hidden in his wristband to pay off his young accomplice. A classic skit was born. I did it years later with my daughter and it worked like a charm then, too. Now whenever a box arrives in the mail my wife tells me to leave the children alone.

One afternoon I rented this absolutely beautiful Vancouver Grizzly outfit I planned on using on the court. It was so pretty that I had to try it at home on the kids first. They were tiny (Griffin was maybe four and my daughter, Mairin, was only three), and I was a little concerned about scaring them. But I couldn't resist. I knew that the kids would drive up with their lovely mom at exactly 3:20 that sunny afternoon. After all, that was their routine.

Despite the heat, I donned the brown grizzly fur and climbed up on the roof, thinking they would all get a chuckle out of driving up to see a big bad bear on the roof. The shingles were baking me. The minutes passed. Soon it was 3:45. What could be keeping them? Better late than never, the car finally rolled up and I knelt in my best mean bear pose. I felt intimidating for sure! My tiny daughter simply looked up, saw me, and said to Colleen, "Mom, why is Dad up on the roof?" The only joke that day was on me.

Speaking of costumes, I once came out as Coyote wearing a short gray beard and gray hair and stripped off my warm-up suit, revealing a trench coat. I sat down next to Ed Bradley. I was fake-arrested while decked out as a fat Jack Nicholson acting out his obvious pro-Lakers bias.

One mayor of San Antonio would hold up a sign saying *Coyote* and an arrow pointing to an empty seat. After a pregnant pause, I would show up with a sign showing an arrow pointing at him that said "Wolff." Nelson Wolff and I did that bit, which ended with the arrows and names being pointed in the right direction, for years.

Another good sport was Tiger Woods. He had just inked a huge multimillion dollar deal with Nike. This was definitely newsworthy and therefore skit-worthy. I learned that he would be in town for the Texas Open and planned to attend a Spurs game. That got my mind racing. What if I showered him with gifts befitting his newfound love affair with Nike? Without warning him ahead of time, I entered the court and presented him with various products that proudly displayed the distinctive Nike swoosh. I produced a headband, a shoe, and a pair of sweatbands—innocuous stuff. Then I raised the ante. I ripped the Nike shirt right off a nearby fan (a plant, of course). I stole a woman's purse that, once turned around, had the trademark swoosh on it, too. I gave each item to Tiger. A Nike toaster was followed by a Nike weedwhacker. He was actually crying with laughter. Then I stripped off my long-sleeved Spurs warm-up suit to reveal that I was Coyote only from the neck up. From my shoulders down, I had on the tiger costume I'd rented that day. The skit was complete.

Contrast that with the same "spontaneous" type of moment I had with one of the American Gladiators. The reckless activities of these huge muscle-bound men and women were then being highlighted by Joe Theismann and Mike Adamle on national TV. They all had names like Nitro or Laser or Zap. Once I found out they would be at a game, I was ready to rumble. I came out decked in a tight leotard and sat down next to Biceps or whatever his nickname was. Without blinking an eye, and despite being on camera in front of thousands of fans, he curtly said, "You so

much as touch me and I'll kill you. Don't touch me."
And you can dress up those two sentences with your
best colorful language if you'd like to add some real-
ism. He'd set me up perfectly. The rest of the skit
would be easy. I held out one finger, paused, and—
as the crowd dared me to—touched him and ran like
a sissy. He never did come after me, all the fans in attendance got a laugh, and that explains why I am
now part of the Witness Protection Program.

Other funny interludes include the time a very
pretty, but drunk, young lady motioned me over and
then whispered in my ear that I had a great #@%
(three-letter word for *derriere*). I was flattered. Only
what she didn't know was that she wasn't comment-
ing on *my* buttocks. The Coyote had this huge piece
of foam in the rear. If not for the fact that I couldn't
speak in costume, I might have been tempted to say,
"Well, if you like my rear end so much, here it is," and
given her the foam insert as a souvenir. I think I was
having fantasies that she would sell it, giving me the
chance to utter the rare phrase, "Hey, honey, my butt
is on eBay."

Once, while in full sprint from the balcony to the
court, I was unexpectedly interrupted by a female

who yelled at the top of her lungs from a restroom doorway that she wanted the Coyote to do certain sexual favors for her. I was in too much of a hurry to pay much attention, so on I ran. Turns out she was buck naked. She was ultimately arrested, after which she kicked out a squad car window. I missed the whole thing, but the guys on our staff kidded me for quite some time about Coyote being such a draw for the ladies. What can I say? Animal magnetism at its best.

FOUR
CRASH

People are like tea bags. You have to put them in hot water before you know how strong they are.

Anonymous

One night I was home alone, in bed. Colleen and the kids were living with her mother while we renovated our house. I hung around to supervise the construction, sleeping in a small room behind our garage. On this particular occasion, I had just returned from one of our successful 2003 play-off games. I had dunked, been passed overhead by fans, improvised my way through numerous hot timeouts, ridden the six-foot unicycle, and hit a half-court shot facing backward. I was spent but content. After I'd cooled off a bit and was lying down, the room started spinning. No pain at all. Just the worst hangover-type feeling I'd ever experienced. And this minus any alcohol!

I was intrigued by what was happening, but I assumed it was from overexertion. What else could it be? The entire episode lasted two minutes, tops. I shrugged it off. I didn't even mention it to my wife.

Must be dehydration, I thought. Heck, with my mascot job, I'd been thirsty since Nixon was president. I was fit, I was firm, I was tough.

And, boy, was I stupid.

I have always thought of myself as a pretty knowledgeable fellow, but I must admit that I'd never heard of a TIA. As I now know, these transient ischemic attacks—temporary shortages of blood flow to areas of the brain—are clear warning signs of an impending stroke. Had I correctly identified the dozen or so episodes that occurred in the two or three months leading up to my stroke, I'm certain I wouldn't be using the backspace key as much as I do today. My commonly uncomfortable lifestyle as Coyote proved to be a double-edged sword: I was keenly aware of my body, but my high threshold for pain and discomfort led me to underestimate what were very serious incidents indeed.

When I did seek medical advice, my doctors were concerned about the attacks, but nobody was thinking stroke. At first, it simply didn't occur to anyone that a forty-seven-year-old fitness freak, a nondiabetic nonsmoker with normal blood pressure and no family history of stroke, would suddenly suffer a stroke. I was being tested for various brain diseases. My wife and I were investigating multiple sclerosis online. Not knowing the exact cause of the dizzy spells caused us to fear the worst.

During one test that involved flooding my ears with warm water, I began to feel really lousy. I knew pain. I knew discomfort. I lived with it all the time. But this was different. This was really sick. This was horrible.

When that test was complete, I was sent to have yet another MRI . . . or was it an MRA? As we waited in the aptly named "waiting room" for what seemed like hours, I was fading fast. My head was drooping more by the minute. I began drooling. Lying in the imaging tube, I tried desperately to fight off a blistering headache.

On the way home I distinctly remember hanging out the car window like a Pomeranian—only this dog was vomiting. Tree branches were hitting me in the face on the two-lane road. I now tell my wife that any time a man is throwing up in his new car, it's a clear sign that an emergency room visit is in order, despite his protests.

Because protest I did. All I could think about was getting home. I had no plan for how to ease my discomfort, but I was convinced that somehow things would settle down once we were there.

Things didn't get much better at home. I'm uncertain of the exact chronology from this point on, but I do recollect Colleen calling my sister, Nancy, in California so that she could convince me to call 911. I imagine that the big stroke had occurred by then. I was just in denial. "Get me some water and I'll be okay," I'd say. "Just give me a minute and this will pass." Nonsense like that.

When I realized my wife was phoning another state for help, I finally agreed to go to the emergency room. But I still refused to go by ambulance. By this time I was in such bad shape that our next-door neighbor had to help Colleen hoist me into the car.

What a car ride that was. I felt so bad that I'm not sure I even realized my right side was immobile. My speech was slurred, but my headache was gone. I was sweating buckets, which I was used to, but there was no furry suit involved. As Colleen drove, her face wet with tears, I briefed her on my life insurance, the computer codes for online banking, and the like.

In the emergency room I couldn't look up or forward without getting nauseated. I remember looking down at the tile floor and seeing my own drool. I must have been a handsome specimen indeed. Come to think of it, I once played Renfield in *Dracula*; this time I must have looked like him for real.

I also remember delivering quite a rant about how my elderly father, who lives in a retirement home nearby, relied on me to bring him groceries and medicines. Who would get these things to him now? In retrospect, my concern about his weekly supply of Diet Coke seems almost comical. Because on that evening, my career ended. I was about to spend weeks in the intensive care unit. I wouldn't see my home for another three months.

I was a stroke victim.

You would think I would know, but I'm not certain when I first noticed I was paralyzed on my right side. There was no sudden realization, at least none that I can remember. It was almost as if I woke up knowing my fate, immediately intent on fixing it.

Nothing on my right side would move. Even that side of my face was droopy. It was as if someone had flicked a switch and turned off that half of my body. This was a new feeling for me; I'd always had great body control. I had to adjust, and quickly.

My athletic and injury-prone background, the very thing that had caused me to ignore the TIAs, was now working for me. Unable to form words, I silently took a physical inventory of my vital organs and knew I would at least survive. All those stunt-filled years had left me with an uncanny knowledge of my body.

Though I was unable to move a finger on my right side, I thought it significant that I could feel the subtle difference between a bare human hand and one covered in a latex glove. The nurses attending me didn't know it, but I felt that was the athletic crack in the dam. I couldn't tell it to anyone at the time, but I figured if I could feel texture differences, the other functions couldn't be far behind. (This belief may or may not have been true, but it suited me.) Weeks went by before I could move my right thumb even one-quarter of an inch, but I was privately pleased to see my hypothesis come true. I demonstrated my thumb accomplishment to everyone within sight of my hospital room. Even paralyzed in bed, I was still showing off, I guess. I used that victory as inspiration to slowly win other battles.

As a kid I once struck out seventeen batters in a six-inning Little League game, and now I couldn't open a packet of Sweet'N Low without using my teeth. But I knew it was a matter of time before I regained the use of my hand. I'd rehabbed all sorts of injuries before. What was one more?

The fact that I was paralyzed didn't much enter my thoughts. Nothing heroic—I just don't remember thinking about anything other than improving. Early on, I privately decided my ultimate goal was to dance again with my daughter, Mairin, then seven years old. We had begun this private tradition years before. Every time we went to the movies, she would grab my hand as the credits began to roll and ask me to dance in an adorably formal British accent. We would sprint to the front of the theater and waltz and twirl with glee. She loved for me to grab both her hands and spin in circles until she was dizzy. I was determined to see the joy on Mairin's face as she danced with Daddy. I made that my recovery target. I'd do extra reps during rehab and think about her for inspiration.

Lying paralyzed, unable to move from my bed, I had a lot of time to think. When I had my stroke, we had just remodeled. I joke that it just about killed me; I was another contractor victim. But those three months or so that I was hospitalized were gut-wrenching. I wanted my trusty bed at home. I wanted to see my kids. I wanted to see if I could ever make it upstairs to the second story we had just completed. Hopes were all I had.

One thing all the doctors and nurses harped on was that improvements are most likely in the first six months after a stroke. This window of opportunity was not about to be ignored by me. I was trying, at least, to use my right side on the second day.

I'm careful, when speaking publicly, to say that if there's one thing I learned about stroke and its recovery, it's that every person reacts differently. My prior physical fitness and training regimen made it easier for me to react positively. Using your bad side as much as you can and attempting rehab shortly after your stroke gives you the best chance at recovery. I don't want to imply that you can have a stroke, do a few exercises, and then drive to an icehouse for a smoothie, good as new. Recovery may still leave you wheelchair-bound or worse. But if you work hard, early, and often, you will know you gave it your very best, whatever the results.

After a few weeks in ICU, I was moved to a regular hospital room and then to a rehabilitation unit. I naturally began to ask about what functions might return and when. I learned that stroke differed from person to person: nothing could be planned out; nothing was certain. I looked at my X-rays, decided my own prognosis, and told the staff what I thought we ought to do. Dr. Story, a learned older gentleman who was consulted about my case, listened carefully to my conjectures and then said, "Well, how about I play the part of the doctor here and you try being the patient?" It wasn't really a question. I was labeled the "impatient patient" from that day on. I had a lot to learn. I wasn't used to sitting down for long periods, let alone being bedridden and half-paralyzed to boot.

Nausea was my biggest hurdle at this point. Any attempt to get vertical resulted in intense vertigo. I moved the bed upward in tiny increments, trying to adjust to being upright again for any length of time. One day I noticed that I could move a toe. At night when others were dreaming, I was constantly wakened by the sensation of muscles "firing" in my right leg. I assumed that the arm, being closer to the heart, would respond sooner. I was surprised when my right leg showed life first. I could, after a time, raise my right leg completely off the bed. Not long afterward I began trying to walk, with dismal results.

In rehab, I was under the watchful eye of Dr. Santos. Knowledgeable and dapper in his Hawaiian shirts, he looks like a blend of the Surgeon General and Magnum, P.I. Since I would feel dizzy and quickly lose my balance after being upright for any period of time, he correctly labeled me a fall risk and ordered that a small orange band be placed on my wrist. I absolutely hated that wristband, though I knew how much I needed it. I have worn wristbands while in character, but this one was different. It was my scarlet letter.

Being somewhat hardheaded, I broke all sorts of house safety rules by trying too much too soon. If I was told to stay in bed until tomorrow, I would simply wait until midnight—considered the next day in a court of law—and begin my own physical trials. The last thing Dr. Santos wanted was for me to add a broken hip to my infirmities. Soon I found that not only was I sporting the fall-risk wristband; I was also grounded in my bed.

Imagine running or lifting weights every day for more than twenty years and suddenly being forced to sit still. I didn't know how to do it. I wanted desperately to start rehabbing something. Hadn't I been jumping off a trampoline just days before? Now it was unsafe for me to try to walk, and that was hard for me to comprehend. I hated the fact that the doctors were right.

I was trying my best to be a good soldier, to take one day at a time. Until.

One night at about midnight I could hear one of the hospital night staff talking about how the Coyote had been hospitalized. I took exception to this immediately. The Coyote was fine; it was I, Tim Derk, who was sick. And then this person proceeded to go on about how easy the mascot life was and how overpaid the Coyote was. "The Coyote?" she said. "He's not all that!" I was just smiling at this point, resigned to the fact that this young lady was simply one of those people who are opinionated but misinformed. Then I heard her say that she could be the Coyote if given the chance. I feel it my duty to tell you that this woman was 320 pounds and probably couldn't spell the word *triathlon*, much less compete in one.

Now I admit that I was under oath to stay in bed. But I dare anyone to listen to talk like that—for the better part of an hour, no less—and take no action. I had yet to receive the word that I could never return to the court, so my determination to get well—beginning that moment—increased tenfold. I'd show her.

I spotted a chair in the corner of the room, perhaps six feet away. I now considered that chair my own Mount Everest. Achieving that goal would prove that I was making progress, that I could even go back to work one day. Despite right-side paralysis, regardless of being heavily sedated with the sleep aid Ambien, I slung myself out of bed with the aim of reaching that summit. In the darkness of my room, I fell in a heap on the tile floor. Still focused on my task, I crawled like a Marine to the chair and triumphantly pulled myself up to sit on it.

Then I realized I had to make the return trip.

Somehow I made it to the bed, but I got hung up on the egg-crate mattress. My attempts to use my good leg for propulsion were defeated by the slippery blue booties on the tile floor. Traction was only a dream. Like a mouse struggling to get out of my own self-made glue trap, I exhausted all my strength. I had no choice but to sit on the cool tile and wait for assistance. My voice, considerably weakened by the stroke, hadn't returned yet. Any cries I could muster were only faint echoes in the hall. Hours passed. I managed to get my good hand on the bedrail, but I lacked the strength to boost myself the rest of the way. Buzzing proved futile. I contemplated hooking the phone cord with my left toes. Prone on my belly, I began throwing objects into the hall in the hopes of drawing some attention. If I could dunk on NBC, I could certainly throw a plastic cup. "Thwack" was the only sound I heard as the cup missed the entry-way and hit the wall in front of me. On the third try, I became a successful "pitcher" by throwing a "pitcher" into the hall. Someone on the night staff finally appeared and asked if I was having any problems, and that was that.

I learned a valuable lesson: broken promises and sleep drugs are a volatile mix. But Everest was now mine. I did make it to the chair. It was returning from the summit that proved to be the hard part.

Over time I mastered the art of walking more than six feet, but I still had to promise to roll myself into the bathroom on a wheelchair. One day Dr. Santos declared that he would cut off the despised fall-risk wristband if I could make it unaided from my bed to

Here I am as Albert in my high school's production of *Bye Bye Birdie*. Theater fans will recall that Dick Van Dyke played him in the 1963 movie. Van Dyke is in my top three people to have lunch with. My appreciation of physical comedy started with him. On the left is my sister, Nancy, the successful sibling.

My freshman year at Trinity University, I spent a lot of time on the tennis courts (note the zinc oxide on my nose). Here my rackets had been strung too tightly and snapped from the strain.

I began playing tennis at the new park down the street from my house when I was a teenager. If they'd built a baseball field I'd probably have taken up baseball instead. Good thing it wasn't a casino. Tennis, and later theater and the Coyote, provided an outlet for all my extra energy.

This is one of the moves I developed while playing Frisbee Golf at Trinity University. I should add that the sport provided an excellent opportunity for sun-tanning—hence, I'm shirtless. Years later, Sean Elliott, whom the Spurs had just drafted, and I toured South Texas to promote the team. We were on a street corner in Laredo when I did this stunt. In an interview with Rich Marini, Elliott recalled, "Coming home from dinner, Tim grabbed this light pole and just raised his body out and up until his feet were pointing to the sky. It was like something from the Cirque du Soleil."

Me shown here as a song-and-dance man in *Cole,* a revue featuring the music of Cole Porter, at Trinity University's Attic Theater in 1983. My performance in this show led to me being asked to experiment as a Spurs mascot.

Early in my career I did a lot of roadwork for the Rockford Lightning, a Continental Basketball Association team in Illinois. I brought the use of stilts to a new level. I was very proud of the furry feet at the bottom.

The first time I set foot on Texas soil, I knew I would marry a woman from Texas. The first time I set eyes on Colleen, I knew she would be the one.

My first time on national TV. Back then, a lot of kids would go to college games and hold up signs for the camera. "Hi, Mom! Send Money" was the most popular one. I thought it would be funny to parody that, and the NBC cameraman agreed.

My children, who had never seen snow, wondered what it felt like to have it fall on you. I guessed that the rest of San Antonio might feel the same way, so I came up with a stunt in which I dropped two small bags of popcorn onto the fans below. People looked up as if to say, "Is that all you've got?" While "Let It Snow" played over the P.A. system, we showered them with three big bags. I made it snow!

Me baking at 350 degrees for twenty minutes until I was done, having failed to rile up my kids. They "bearly" noticed me on the roof.

The Alexis Brothers were a well-known duo, one big and one little gentleman, who appeared at halftime once. As part of their act, the larger would lift the smaller, using just one of his muscular arms. One would lift the other with his leg. For my parody of this feat of strength I had a coyote doll duct-taped to my legs.

If I hadn't become the Coyote, this is probably what I would have looked like on my way to the office.

Here is Coyote shooting Spurs shirts into the stands with an air compressor. In the early days, the T-shirt cannon weighed ninety pounds, with the tank. It was strapped on, and I used to feel as if I was running around with a huge Sony TV on my back. In contrast, the version now in use weighs five pounds. Mascots are no longer allowed to shoot into the upper deck due to concerns about fan safety. In the old days at the Alamodome I used to bet the sound guy that I could shoot one right into his sound booth (and I did). It's amazing how much excitement "the gun" brings to a timeout. I've seen men knock over ladies in wheelchairs to get a $3 T-shirt.

Slam-dunking is an NBA mascot's stock in trade. In this shot, I've sprung from a mini-trampoline to achieve this height. When the Spurs hosted the NBA All-Star Game in 1996, I won the Mascot Slam Dunk competition—blind-folded.

This skit was inspired by a UPS delivery. The ref has just opened an unexpected Christmas present from Coyote. My five-year-old daughter, Mairin, was the surprise.

I tell my son that he will no doubt be hearing this story at his wedding rehearsal dinner: how Daddy had the brilliant idea of recruiting four-year-old Griffin for a Christmas skit—and ended up being completely upstaged.

Thanks to a brave recruit who lent me his uniform, I was able to pull off one of my all-time favorite impromptu stunts. I joined this group of men and women from Lackland Air Force Base in my usual guise. We were having a good time, but when I stripped off my jersey to reveal the uniform underneath, they burst into cheers.

Yet another example of why I had the highest life insurance premiums in the NBA.

When the Spurs won the 1999 NBA championship, almost 300,000 fans showed up for the celebratory parade on the San Antonio River. I rode on the first barge and dangled a six-foot salmon on a fishing rod over the water every so often. Nothing says "comedy" like a giant fish.

I incorporated the first NBA trophy into more than one skit and built one of my video skits around a poker game in which Coyote slaps this trophy on the table as his final bet.

In one skit I would start by holding up cards for the crowd to read, printed with the words *Yeah!* for the home team and *Boo!* for our opponents. A child would run out and tug on my shirttails, pantomiming "Can I have an autograph?" Coyote would reluctantly stop to sign the autograph, the kid would run off, and I'd resume the routine. Another child would run out, this time asking for a hug. Same reluctance and compliance, then back to the cards. When a third kid ran out, asking for a hug, Coyote was clearly exasperated. After this child—my son, Griffin—got his hug and turned to go, Coyote gave him a playful smack on the butt with his foot. Griffin turned around and clocked Coyote, to the delighted howls of the crowd. We ended the skit with me scooping Griffin into my arms. When we reprised the skit a few years later with my daughter, Mairin, she ripped Coyote's eyes off!

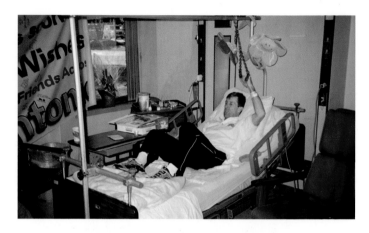

Here I am with the infamous bar that I worked so hard to finally grab. I'm cheating—I have it in my left hand. At that point I couldn't move my right arm at all.

Two fellow members of the "furternity" of NBA mascots, Atlanta's Skyhawk and Harry the Hawk. They have on the "TD" armband my fellow mascots wore in my honor when I was out of commission after my stroke. It meant a lot to me to know my peers had done that. They all signed their armbands and sent them to me, too.

the bathroom. I had to do it five times in a row without failure. It was my Olympic moment. Under his watchful gaze, with the physical therapist spotting me, I got the gold medal.

I was given a single-striped, karate-type cloth belt that my therapist spotters used religiously to hold me up and steady. I wore that belt at all times during the day. I soon felt like a puppy, as the therapists walked behind me holding my new "leash on life." I wore the belt to occupational therapy and physical therapy. If I dared venture to the bathroom, the lifeline was there. During my physical therapy sessions, I walked in front of the staffers, who would give me little shoves that caused me to lose my footing. Forced to recover my equilibrium, I was thus made to work on balance. I referred to this as my "Malik Rose" exercise because of how Malik loved contact on the court when he was a Spur. Being jostled at work and having no peripheral vision in the Coyote suit was now working for me, and my balance improved dramatically. I never mentioned it—and I'm not really sure I know what irony is—but it felt ironic to go from dunking high in the air and landing on a mat to being asked to try a simple walk across a mat without falling.

Along with physical and occupational therapy, I received cognitive therapy. Much care was taken to determine the damage to my brain from the lack of oxygen during my stroke.

No doubt I was muddled at best, but I felt cerebrally functional. I was dying to prove it to the doctors and technicians. In one of the first cognitive tests, a therapist asked me a series of questions. Being competitive in nature, I was eager to do well and impress her.

"Who is the President?"

I got that one no problem.

"How many eyes does a person have?"

I thought a bit. Then I said, "A man has two eyes normally, but four if you're a professional mascot wearing a foam head."

The therapist didn't even crack a smile.

"What are the names of your children?"

Again I answered correctly.

By now I could see that the therapist was putting

a nice clean check mark by each question I answered correctly. I was proud of that.

"What's the difference between a pencil and a pen?"

I answered that a pencil was temporary but a pen's ink was permanent. I received another easy check for that one.

Then the therapist said, "What's the difference between a house and an apartment?"

"A house is something you buy, and an apartment is something you rent." Nothing but checks on my page so far.

"How old are you?"

"Thirty-seven," I said confidently.

The therapist paused. "How old are you?" she said again.

I said that I was thirty-seven years old. And I watched her put a big bold "X" next to the question. She shook her head in sympathy for the poor stroke patient.

I couldn't convince her of it, but the fact that I had gotten the question wrong had nothing to do with the stroke. I'd lied to the media about my age for so many years that I had no idea how old I really was. I had convinced myself that I was my real age minus ten years.

My pat answers to the media were always the same. To the question of where I went to college, I answered, "Acme University." When asked where I lived, I said, "A den outside Loop 1604." And when asked my age, I replied, "Mid-thirties, but I'm ancient in dog years."

I laughed as the therapist stared at me blankly. I knew no one could understand but a fellow incognito mascot. Now whenever anyone asks me my age, I pause before I answer.

My upper body needed a lot of work. And I needed patience, not my strongest personality trait. The rehab bed had a triangle of steel suspended from a beam that ran the length of the bed. That triangle faced me most of the time, swinging in the breeze, taunting me. I couldn't even raise my right arm high enough to swing that target.

Using my good arm, I elevated my right arm and placed it on the bar. I was sure it would stay up once I released it. Wrong! My bad arm lost all grip and fell like a sack of potatoes on the bed. Undaunted, I attempted this maneuver every two minutes for weeks. While others slept, I stayed awake for hours trying. I just wanted to hit the bottom of that steel triangle with my bad arm and make it sway in the medicine-flavored breeze. I felt I had it in me. It was just a matter of when I could achieve it.

Eventually I got it. I could hit the bar. Trying for more, I used my able hand to lift my right arm to the bar. I let go as I had done countless times before. The hand stayed up. I felt as much pride as any Cirque du Soleil trapeze performer might after mastering an intricate trick.

Interestingly, it wasn't until weeks later that I could grab the bar. I pawed at it initially, but once my brain relearned the curling motion associated with gripping there was no stopping me. I began to feel the texture of the grip portion of the bar: the metal had these delightful little dimples made for keeping the hand from sliding. The steel soon felt cold in my hand.

I proudly sat with my right hand hanging in the air, even during meals, reveling in my newfound talent. At night I could (and still can) feel muscles rejuvenating and firing in my hand, arm, and leg on the right side. I was progressing. And it all began with raising my arm. I was no lawyer, but I had passed my own version of the bar.

Physical therapists are heroic professionals who dedicate themselves to helping people recover from devastating injuries. For months, I watched PTs work with stroke victims, amputees, and the frail elderly. They were there to help every patient achieve his or her personal best. Their patience, their grace under pressure—unbelievable. If there's an HOV lane into heaven, these guys deserve a permanent pass.

To the often depressed and angry patient, however, the therapists' demands can be taxing. It's their job to push you and tire you out. In hindsight you might see that their intentions were nothing but good, but in the heat of the moment you're not always exactly . . . appreciative, let us say.

Amelie Mahoney-Martin and Kathy Schwartz are known as "physical terrorists," an unfair but fitting title that accurately describes what they put their patients through. I grew to know both of these young women well, as I worked with them twice a day for hour after exhausting hour. Under Dr. Santos's supervision, their job was to maximize my results by driving me to maximum effort. A perfect match: I wanted more each day, and they were prepared to give it.

When I began physical therapy, my right hand couldn't even get a reading on the "pinch gauge," a device that measures grip strength. For weeks, the seemingly simple task of touching my right thumb to my pinkie was impossible. During sessions with Kathy, she made me use my right hand exclusively. Even Dr. Santos got into the act: he ordered my left hand bound to my chest during rehab. I couldn't cheat even if I wanted to. I fought to pinch an ordinary plastic clothespin and place it on a string about waist high. Using aggression that had formerly been reserved for City League Softball, I struggled daily.

I spent hours with Amelie trying to pick metal bolts and screws out of a box full of rice in what amounted to a kind of digital torture, designed to improve my dexterity. I wasn't allowed to peek. Nuts and bolts actually felt heavy in my right hand. I'd gone from rearranging the tool room in my garage one day to being unable to pick up a screw the next— and for months to follow.

Of the pair, Amelie was the softie. She just oozed compassion. Or so I thought, until I graduated from the box-of-rice task. I, who could once make a basket while riding a unicycle, cried visible tears as I repeatedly failed to pick up an ordinary house key. The key was on the table in front of me, but my right hand shook uncontrollably. Tears dripped onto the tabletop, and Amelie spurred me on. I tried in vain to hold my hand still enough to attempt a feeble grab. During one of my shakes I accidentally knocked the key to the floor. I sat back, exhausted. Surely sweet Amelie would get it for me. She simply looked at me. "Sorry, but you dropped it, so you pick it up" was written all over her face. I spent the next twenty minutes trying to pick up that metal monster from the slippery floor. I only succeeded when I cheated and braced the key against my shoe.

I had someone massage my injured hand every chance I could. I so wanted to make a fist. When I finally could, it was a slow proposition. My hand felt, and still feels, as if it were swollen or frozen, which makes quick moves impossible no matter how hard I try. I thank God every day that I was born left-handed. I didn't have to learn to write again. To brush my teeth—what a chore that would be. But what I did do before the stroke (and quite proficiently, if I may say so myself) was toss a Frisbee using my off hand. Despite the many physical hurdles I have managed to overcome, I still cannot get my right hand to open fast enough to throw an ordinary disc.

My right side physicality was gone. My balance was shot. My strength had disappeared overnight. I could handle all three of these things. I didn't dare mention it to anyone else, but my greatest fear was that my sense of humor was gone, too. What I had counted on most was taken from me in a flash. I was the proverbial giraffe with a sore throat. To this day, I don't know if my ability to be amused returned on its own or if the world just became funnier as I progressed. But I hated those days when everything seemed grim. It was then that I reached my low point, the real depression that often accompanies a stroke.

I was forced to take antidepressants for months. I knew they were medically necessary, and I was okay with that. But I did not appreciate some of the side effects caused by the mood-altering drug.

Paranoia crept in. I felt it. I heard my wife whooping it up in the next room one night. She was drinking, laughing, and having a grand old time without me. I was certain it was her, but of course it wasn't. One day I explained to my doctors that, as an athlete, I had always tried to use as little medication as possible. I said I worked best with a clean baseline so I could monitor my progress without being doped up by a mixture of medicines. And not only that, the best way to get me undepressed was to give me my manhood back. (Impotence being another nasty side effect.) Against their wishes, I discontinued the antidepressants and watched carefully for the mood swings that might result. I made the right choice, and once functional again I became downright giddy.

My personal recipe for rehab success is basic:

1. Mix three cups of determination, intense exercise, and good medical supervision.
2. Add a pinch of being already physically fit.
3. Then add two-thirds of a cup of good luck.
4. Bake for six months at any temperature.

FIVE
BABY STEPS

Comedy is tragedy plus time.
Carol Burnett

I walked gingerly out of the rehab hospital and headed for the car. I was still using a cane, but walking upright was a triumph. It had been three months since my last car ride with Colleen.

Surprisingly, she didn't head straight home. She drove to Seguin, to the home of a family who breeds puppies. The parents, both cancer survivors, had heard of my plight and developed an email-based friendship with my wife while I was bedridden. This great family wanted to help, and Colleen had accepted their offer of a brand-new puppy, free of charge.

Our new "Labradoodle," a cross between a

Labrador and a poodle, would learn the ropes at home along with me. While I relearned how to tie my shoes and button my shirt, she'd be at my side with that infectious puppy enthusiasm. She would struggle with house-training while I struggled with the notion of trying to put a sock on my foot with my good hand.

Once we did reach our house, I walked independently from the car. By this time, I was fiercely dizzy from being upright for so long. My wife, expecting me to head for the bed in the front room as the doctor had ordered, was no doubt surprised (and probably a little shocked) when I made my way to the steps that led upstairs. I hadn't mentioned it to anyone, but I had wondered for weeks if I could ever walk upstairs on my own again. My kids weren't home, but their rooms were up there and I wanted to be able to tuck them in at night. It wasn't the prettiest trek, but I made it to the top on my own power. I cried tears of joy mixed with embarrassment that I had to work so hard to do something so simple.

Back downstairs, I noticed the banners, cards, letters, and flowers that filled the entryway of the house. Over ten thousand emails from nineteen countries had arrived. It was overwhelming. I even received a touching yet unnerving handmade card signed by prison convicts. David Hasselhoff is famous in Germany and I'm big in the state pen.

I arose at seven the next morning, eager to begin my rehab training. At first I was confused and dazed. Colleen was concerned that I'd get lost if I traveled too far, so I simply walked the block in front of my house, over and over. In short order I had enough stamina to go around the block. However, my right leg would lock painfully with every step. I worked hard on stopping that. Hills were murder. I remember hitting my hand repeatedly on the cell phone in my right pocket each time I attempted a stride. I had to learn to increase the distance I held out my hand while my bad arm was learning to swing. I concentrated on every other step in order to avoid stubbing my toe. Soon I had my daily regimen in place.

Working out during the day was, thankfully, nothing new to me. I had done it for decades at work, and I took on this new job with a vengeance. I began each morning by walking the block once or twice. I'd rest my leg for a few minutes. Then I headed to the back room and began the stationary bike, pedaling at a maniacal pace. (I gradually worked my way up to an hour.) Sometimes I'd pedal using only my right leg. After working my legs, I'd scramble to the floor and pedal some more with my arm, putting just my right hand on the pedal. I'd work on my upper-body strength and stamina for fifteen minutes this way.

I also wanted to get my singing voice back. I was always a belter when it came to singing—never terrifically melodic but strong voiced and character filled. And I never sang a note that was off-key. The stroke changed all that. My speaking voice was flat and uninteresting; my singing voice was truly dreadful. I couldn't stay on pitch to save my soul. I took it upon myself to see if I couldn't do something about that. I figured that as long as I was pedaling a bike several hours a day, I might as well use that time to work on my singing. Pedaling like a madman, I'd make my best effort to stay on pitch. I sang along to the CD player blaring loudly enough to drown me out—should anyone happen to pass by. I managed to sing for nearly an hour a day during that first summer. Now that's what I call multitasking.

Then it was outside for a session with Therabands, the thick rubber bands that are indispensable for post-stroke resistance training. I had tied the bands to the column of my back porch, and I'd do three sets of 15 before heading to the rehab facility, where I'd learn even more new drills. I really looked forward to checking my grip strength on the pinch gauge. At first I registered a meager two pounds of squeeze pressure. Eventually I reached over 100 on the grip scale, right before graduating from rehab.

Back home after rehab workouts, I would rest my shaky limbs a bit. Then it was back to walking, stationary biking, hand pedaling, and Therabands once again. After my second home workout of the day, I threw a basketball against the side of the house and tried catching it using my right hand only. Colleen knew where I was by the thumping she could hear through the walls. I finished up with another, usually longer, walk. Then I was done until the next day, when I would begin it all again. Rest was important for rehab, too—although my wife will tell you that I only rested when she ordered me to.

In those early days, I was slothlike. I could move, but everything was slow. I felt how I imagined a prizefighter must feel after being punched in the head when he isn't looking. I was a fighter in the ring, and I had definitely lost the first round. I was confused but had my wits enough to know that fact. My eyesight was affected, too. Everything was hazy. An eye specialist who focused on treating stroke victims explained that he could prescribe me expensive glasses but my vision would most likely improve over time. (He was proved correct after four months or so.) I had this god-awful ringing in my ears twenty-four hours a day, seven days a week, for months. Try sleeping soundly with someone ringing your doorbell all day and night. I hated it. Although that, too, went away.

It was during this period that I went from being tirelessly driven to appreciating slow and steady progress. For example, before the stroke I'd come home after a game and explain that, yes, I had made a backward half-court shot that night in front of thousands, but it wasn't a swish. I could do better. During rehab, I concentrated first on my toes, then my fingers, then my speech. I learned that little victories ultimately provide their own impressive graph of improvement.

Baby steps were the key, once again.

That was the utilitarian approach Gregg Popovich had always preached. As head coach of the Spurs, Pop reminded his players that the season was long and hard. He believed that the key to success in a hard season was persistence and consistent play. His analogy was a rock, which might remain unaffected by the first blows of a pick hammer. But if you kept wielding that hammer (playing hard and working on defense every night), the rock would eventually chip and then break under the constant pressure (as would your opponent).

His advice was proved right when we won our first NBA title using that credo. The 1999 championship ring—which the Spurs were nice enough to present to me, too—is inscribed with the picture of a small hammer banging on a large rock that has been successfully cracked. It's on the ring for all to see, but few know its real meaning.

Little did I know then that the hammer would again be a pivotal tool in my life. One of the physical therapists showed me a simple yet effective drill to measure progress in my recovery. The idea is to take an ordinary hammer and see how long, and how still, you can hold it with the head in the nine o'clock position. I did this using my right arm. I had no idea how heavy a hammer could be. Furniture making was clearly not in my future.

I was instructed to begin by holding the hammer up near the head and to gradually, over time, work my hand down until I could hold the very end of the handle. I worked on it endlessly. I even had a hammer with me in bed when I slept.

Early in my hammer marathon, Colleen walked into the room and saw me brandishing my trusty training tool. It was my first attempt at holding up the weight by grasping the end of the handle. She was kind and applauded my earnest efforts. She also remarked how good it was to see my hand go up and down like I was pounding an imaginary nail. I chuckled and thanked her, admitting that the shaking motion was unintentional. I was actually trying to hold the hammer still.

Neighbors would often drive by our house with a carpool of small children saying, "There's Mr. Derk. He's on the front porch again, holding up his hammer." I often think of Pop and his philosophy when I remember my own "hammer time."

I needed to remind myself of what I had overcome, especially when it came to conquering the dreaded "stroke circle." When I walked, my left leg would bend normally or stay in a straight line when I wanted it to. My right leg, however, wanted badly to go in a counter-clockwise horizontal loop. And my right knee locked painfully with every step. The muscles needed to be reprogrammed so that they'd know how far to extend and how to walk straight. As I practiced keeping the path of my right foot as straight as the edge of the line of Mexican tiles in my den, I remembered the endless tennis drills of my youth. As before, when hitting a tennis ball against a wall, I practiced endlessly. Even now, I occasionally bang into a doorway and my wife will notice my "faux paw" of coordination. On the street I walk by listening to my steps. I try desperately to keep from dragging my right toe. I have to think constantly when walking. If I don't, it shows.

After being home for a month, I was able to walk fairly briskly. One day, a funny thought popped into my head. What if I simply leaned forward and tried to run? I had an awful gait at first. In fact, it was so embarrassing that for a while I ran only when hidden by the dark of night or in the privacy of my backyard, using the uneven surface of the grass to test my balance. Over the next few weeks, as I improved my run, I went public. Running the sidelines at my daughter's soccer games, I'd hold up my trusty hammer.

As a former marathoner, I saw running as an important milestone. I began to meet our WNBA mascot at a local college track, where we ran for time. Never judgmental, the mascot would run with me. He saw me fall on my first attempt at a mile, when that dreaded right toe just wouldn't cooperate. Eventually I worked my way up to a 6:52 mile with his encouragement. We tossed a medicine ball together. We played pitch and catch. I was trying new things, and my whole outlook improved along with my body.

Before I leave you with that "and everybody lived happily ever after" feeling, I must tell you about the annual Spurs Christmas party, one year post-stroke. The party was held at a bowling alley where scores are automatically posted on overhead projectors for all to see. My prestroke best was 256 with ten strikes. My best score in costume was 172. I felt pretty good, so I was eager to see what I might bowl. In my first frame, I knocked over one pin and then rolled a gutter ball. I stood at the end of the lane, transfixed, feeling as if I was trying to bowl on a cruise ship in bad weather. I ended up with a ten-frame score of 66.

My loss of balance was made painfully evident. I've had to resign myself to the fact that I'm 20 percent of the tennis player I once was. All thoughts of one day retiring to a life as a teaching pro at a quaint bed-and-breakfast or posh hotel are gone. For medical reasons, I'm not allowed to do many of the things I prided myself on before. I even have to avoid climbing ladders.

I still suffer from shakiness in my stroke hand. It took me forever to relearn how to type. At first I couldn't even see the monitor clearly enough to read. On my first attempt at typing, I placed my hands on the keyboard with what I thought was a ginger touch. Suddenly there were eighteen L's on the paper. I would swear that I hadn't moved a muscle, but my shaky right hand was hitting the home row key and I didn't even know it.

And my emotional thermostat is markedly off. I can't watch *Old Yeller*. I cry often. I get angry suddenly. I laugh inappropriately.

Soon after I returned to work, I was in a meeting with coworkers when some controversy developed.

Nothing big, but one of my colleagues made me feel a little underappreciated. All of a sudden, I was acting like a four-year-old whose favorite toy has just been taken away. I began sobbing and expounding on how hard I was trying. Between sobs, I explained that it was the stroke talking and asked everyone to ignore me. To my amazement, they did. Much to their credit, they've never brought it up again. I'm working on regulating these emotional flare-ups. It's a work in progress. It's all part of the brain healing process.

There is no doubt that a stroke patient's life changes dramatically. How you deal with the change is the only thing you can control. Rather than dwell on what I've lost, I choose to focus on what I have to be grateful for. I am truly thankful for all those who helped me improve. Many people and events have inspired me. I read hundreds of letters addressed to me each night for further inspiration.

I had it explained to me this way: I can light a fire, which could inspire you to get off the couch. But it's you who actually decides whether to move or to continue watching TV. You eventually motivate yourself when you're good and ready.

I had one big payoff for all my hard work a few months after I returned home from the rehab facility. Two repairmen arrived to replace the heater under my house. I could hear one whisper to the other that I was the Spurs Coyote who'd had a stroke. I felt obligated to say that I *had been* the Coyote. "You don't do it anymore. How come?" the second worker asked. Realizing that he knew nothing of my story, I simply said I'd experienced some health problems in the past year. "My partner told me," he said. Then he added something I'd never heard before, something that made my heart sing. "I'm glad you recovered from your mild stroke," he said. Mild stroke! I knew there was nothing mild about vertebral artery malfunction, but that moment marked a milestone for me. It was the first time I had indeed fooled a stranger. I almost called Dr. Santos right then and there. Now I get a kick out of fooling people regularly.

Near the six-month anniversary of my stroke, I returned to the residential rehab facility where I'd worked so intensively every morning and afternoon. I was eager to show Amelie, my occupational therapist, and Kathy, the physical therapist, how much I'd improved.

While I was there I saw a man crying in a wheelchair. I could sense a mix of depression and knowledge that recovery was going to be a long and arduous process. His name was Nathan. He was a cop who had been ambushed and shot outside a restaurant. Seeing him was like looking into a time-machine mirror. He looked like what I felt like back when I first started. I walked up to Nathan and introduced myself. His speech was disjointed and slurred, but I listened as best I could and told him it was an honor to meet him. Judging by my own amnesia, I'm certain he doesn't remember our meeting. I told him point blank that some people say they know how you feel but are just guessing, but I knew exactly how he felt because I'd been in the exact same place only months before. I told him to hang in there and listen to Kathy and Amelie. He cried some more. I encouraged him to try his hardest and prayed at home that he did. I later heard that he walked out of the rehab facility under his own power. A hero.

SIX
LETTING GO

To reveal art and conceal the artist
is art's aim.

Oscar Wilde

I'm probably one of the only heterosexual men you'll ever meet who has come out of the closet.

People have a hard time understanding why associating the least hint of a human identity with the Coyote disturbed me so deeply. Coyote, in all his joyful goofiness, was a superbly comical, larger-than-life character with no cares in the world. He even walked differently than I did, spinning around three times in a tight circle (like a Labrador would) before sitting down. I passionately believed that the success of my creation depended on an elaborate illusion that permitted fans not to think about the guy underneath the fur. For more than twenty years, I went to fanatical lengths to guard the secret of Coyote's identity.

One day while I was still in the ICU, I had just ventured into the hall for my first solo power walk, my trusty walker as my guide. My hair was disheveled, since I had no right hand to help comb it. I slumped over, concentrating on the enormously difficult task of putting one foot in front of another while remaining upright. I think I probably had more than a passing resemblance to a homeless person.

Even in my confused, brain-damaged state I recognized the shutterlike click of a cell phone camera. Another patient's visitor had scored: "Live at ten! Real-life photos of Coyote down and out!" My sister, Nancy, and Colleen led me back to my room and insisted that I face the inevitable. "It's going to get out one way or another," Nancy declared.

I didn't want to be a part of the rumor mill. I could see myself in the *Star* being secretly married to Britney Spears within the week. I put up moderate resistance, but there really was nothing to do but release the correct information. I couldn't think of any-thing I wanted less, but I had no choice.

That evening, when I looked up at the TV, it was to see tape of Colleen holding a news conference. The newspaper featured a photograph of the two of us, and it was my name I heard on the airwaves of KISS Radio instead of AC/DC. All I could think of was the fact that my marvelous creation, the product of two decades' worth of my best inventive efforts, was being dealt a mortal blow. I cried all night.

In this dark moment, my memories of the extreme lengths I'd gone to to hide my real identity seemed to mock me. There was the time I signed a hundred or so autographs for an hour at a local store. The tabletop was wet from the perspiration that dripped through the fur on my arms, so you can imagine the heat I was feeling inside. After the appearance, the store manager led me to a little room upstairs where I could get a drink and towel off—something I badly needed to do. I entered the room to find it filled with eager employees, all ready to see me re-move my head and reveal my identity. The manager handed me a slip of paper asking if I minded signing a few more autographs before I left. Without taking off the head, and forgoing that badly needed liquid intake, I stayed another forty minutes and signed inscriptions to all sixty-eight names on the list. I then walked out of the store in costume. They never got to see who I was. Anonymity was that important to me.

Then there was the time I had to change into my costume at a McDonald's. The Coyote was still earning his wings, so to speak. I performed for an hour and returned to the restroom stall I had changed in, only to discover that my clothes had been mistaken for trash and thrown out. Still in costume, I had to scale a wall behind the parking lot and dig through the trash to find my people clothes. I felt a little like Superman, only I was changing clothes in a dumpster.

When my cover was blown I understood what had to be done, but that didn't mean I had to like it. This one pill was tough for me to swallow.

Even Colleen couldn't understand why I refused to read any newspaper clippings, why I would begin crying when I heard my name on television. She thought going public with my plight had its pluses. Without a doubt, all the prayers and well wishes did help. My boss, Russ Bookbinder, thought it was difficult for the public to pray when they didn't know who they were praying for. It was time for me to think of them in spite of my own feelings. He was correct.

I'm glad now that I came out of the closet as I did. I appreciate all the kindness I received and truly understand its power.

Which brings us to the more than ten thousand emails and countless cards I received while I was in the hospital and the rehab unit. Colleen was eager to read this correspondence to me, but I withdrew. I didn't want to be reminded of the people I was letting down. I belonged out there, entertaining, and being sick in the hospital was like a failure. Or at least that's the way I felt at first.

Eventually I let myself learn to love those kind words. I used the letters to get me through the hard times, to make me pedal that stationary bike a little bit longer, a little harder. No one else was in that tiny room behind my garage. But I could feel the care of all those thousands of people who had written to me. I wasn't about to let them down.

Nearly three-quarters of the emails I got were from women. They thanked me for affecting their children positively. The Coyote had brought families into the arena. I felt like Sally Field at the Oscars. Kind words came from radio sportscaster Bill Schoening, sports columnist Buck Harvey, sports anchors Don Harris and Greg Simmons, radio show hosts Trey Ware and Chris Duel, and sportscasters Sean Elliott and Steve Kerr, who both once played for the Spurs. On and on. All were much appreciated. I'll never forget.

When I learned that my fellow NBA mascots had worn black armbands emblazoned with "TD" to their home games while I was sick, I lost it. My "furternity" brothers were offering me the ultimate sign of respect. It's one thing to be told by your employer or a fan that you've done a good job. It's something else entirely to be recognized by your peers.

This outpouring of well wishes was amazing. And the thanks I have for the care taken of my wife and family could fill the AT&T Center. My wife is amazing, and she never wavered. But I think the support she got from the Spurs and from the city surely helped. Colleen is San Antonio born and bred. After this experience, she is cemented into this town forever. With good reason, I say.

Grounded in my bed in rehab, it was weeks before I could bring myself to watch the Spurs on TV. I started by glancing at away games on television. I got to the point where I could watch a whole game, as long as it was away, without too much distress. I wasn't supposed to be at those games.

The first home game after Valentine's Day was the first home game I missed in twenty-one years. My unbroken streak of 984 home games was smashed with a vengeance.

It took me a while to tune into home games. At first I would tear up, overwhelmed by despair, and change the channel. But my love for the Spurs overcame my grief, and I found myself watching them play on their home court, too.

I was ready to pay any price to be back with the team. I remember thinking I might have been a good soldier—probably dead, from volunteering to charge up that hill, but a decorated corpse. Anything for the team.

Being as stubborn and hardheaded as I am, it took me a while to realize that it was all over. The notion that I would never don the Coyote head again was hard for me to accept. One doctor in particular was determined to make me understand that medical clearance for mascot work was not going to happen.

Just the name Dr. Diana Ballesteros, one of the handful of docs who took care of me, brings a huge smile to my face. Retirement was still a dirty word to me when Dr. Ballesteros, a straight shooter, explained what had happened in my stroke. The vertebral artery makes a two-pronged fork, shaped like the letter Y, in the back of the skull. A piece of mine on the left side broke off and flew up into my head, cutting off the blood supply to the brain. The clot was too high to chase with surgery and later dissolved, but the damage was done. I had lost the things I used the most when entertaining. Balance and coordination had been my lifelong friends. We were total strangers in an instant.

The good news, of course, was that only one side of the two-pronged fork was destroyed. Given time, and the proper stimulation through rehab, other blood vessels in the brain would compensate for those lost. They might take over some of the motor functions lost when the left side of my artery failed.

The bad news was that I only had one prong of that fork working now. I was driving cross-country with no spare tire. To hear the doc tell it, bocce ball and backgammon were about the only games I could safely play now. We went through all the sports I'd played in the past and the risk of taking up any one of them again.

Dr. Ballesteros got me to understand how impossible it would be for me to return to the court. That was tough to hear. She convinced me that I would never get to ski with my son. "What about unicycling?" I asked. She laughed.

I guess I've finally learned that, in fact, the show doesn't always have to go on. Caring for my family and myself is important, too. When I finally accepted the fact that my career was over, I began to think about the fans again. Thousands of people were counting on me to recover. I wasn't going to let them down.

SEVEN
SURROUNDED BY EAGLES

If you want to soar like an eagle,
don't hang around with the turkeys.

Walter Derk

The Spurs have always been like a small family. In the early days we had a drive-through ticket window, and when it came time to send out the season tickets all the employees (a dozen of us or so) would assemble to get the job done: everybody around a long table, with one person licking the envelopes, one stamping, one grouping them by zip code, and so on. The staff has grown more than twentyfold since I started, but the philosophy is the same. I never had to lie about the Spurs when talking to the media. It's all good, and it's all true.

We have had, and continue to have, some truly great players: Avery Johnson, Sean Elliott, David Robinson, Steve Kerr, Malik Rose, Tim Duncan, Manu Ginobili, Tony Parker—I could go on. Every one of these men is not only talented with a Spalding but also approachable and amiable. It's an honor to know them. And the same holds true for our management. I feel privileged to work with the people I do. The Holt style of taking care of employees and fans has not gone unnoticed: in 2004 ESPN recognized the Spurs as the number one team in all of professional sports.

Knowing that I had a job and that my place in the Spurs family was secure played a big part in my recovery. Sure, I had worked for the company for most of my adult life by the time I got sick. I still knew how easy it would have been for them to say, "You were great. Thanks! Now don't let the door hit you on the way out."

But they created a position for me—Manager of Mascot Development. It's the job I do to this day. I've been called "Mr. Miyagi" from *Karate Kid*. I corral all three of the Spurs Sports & Entertainment mascots:

the Coyote for the NBA, the Silver Fox for the WNBA, and T-Bone, our bull for AHL hockey. I'm proud to say that we've assembled a fine group of hard-working young men who, combined, need less Bengay than I did.

Back when I started, Henry Cisneros was mayor, Tim Duncan was home fast asleep in his crib, and Tony Parker was just a sonogram. Now that someone else is donning the suit, I see for the first time the smiles that the Coyote brings. I grin at his antics. I really had no idea that running around in brown footie pajamas would bring people so much joy.

I admit to being lousy at spectator sports. I'd much rather be inside the action on the field. My first season watching from the sidelines was 2005. Even though it was the third time the Spurs won an NBA championship, I didn't know how to act. I'd never been part of a championship celebration as a human! But I did know how hard all our staff worked all year long. To see them crying with joy and reveling in the team's success was a new pleasure.

Driving home through celebratory traffic on the night of the championship game, I glanced to my right and saw a night-time security guard jumping up and down and talking, no doubt, about the team winning it all, on his cell phone.

The Spurs might knock you down on a hard drive to the basket, but then we smile and politely help you up. Owner Peter Holt's philosophy of family and fun, Head Coach Gregg Popovich's emphasis on discipline, and day-to-day boss Russ Bookbinder's work ethic have proven a perfect mix. Good guys do finish first.

Angelo Drossos owned the team when I first signed on. Drossos was a true visionary; he foresaw what the Coyote could and would become. He was a plain speaker, and you either liked that or you didn't. I liked it.

After three years as the Coyote, I announced to the team that I was retiring to attend business school at the University of Texas. One day Angelo invited me to meet him for lunch. The NBA season was approaching. I agreed to the meal but told him up front that I was not to be swayed from my desire to become a Longhorn graduate. He assured me that we were just meeting socially. At lunch, I told him how excited I was about school and about my new life in Austin. I knew he was just buying time until he could persuade me to return as the team mascot.

As I spoke, he began sliding me scribbled numbers on a napkin. Each time he offered the napkin to me, I'd simply push it back in his direction. This seesaw war of paper products finally ended when I stared at one last napkin and put it in my back pocket. I thanked him for lunch, returned to Austin, and called U-Haul. There was no stopping Angelo when he made up his mind to get something. I headed back to San Antonio—the smartest thing I ever did (well, maybe third smartest, after proposing to my wife and getting TiVo). Deep down, he knew I was born to perform, and he was willing to give me the stage I wanted so much. After 1,100 games, 5,000 appearances, 100 TV shows, and 5 countries, I wouldn't change a thing.

I was working in sports, and I was working with children. I was making people laugh while not going so far as to throw my shoes out the window, as I'd done in fourth grade. I was where I belonged. I often arose moaning and hurting from exertion, but I can honestly say it never felt like work. And each outing allowed me to meet some extraordinary people.

While I was in ICU, unable to lift one finger on my right side, former Spurs star David Robinson and his wife, Valerie, were among the first to visit. They sat with me for some time. I slurred my speech and lay motionless on my right side, but David patiently listened to every word. Having seen him handle his own retirement with such class and dignity, I was (almost) ready to accept my own unforeseen retirement. We conversed in terms that I could understand—athlete to athlete, dad to dad. He talked about how watching from a seat in the second row felt uncomfortable at first but got better with time. He pointed out that I would enjoy more time with my family now, since I had previously worked nearly every weekend. While it was true that I had to be the one to ultimately accept change gracefully, it was certainly easier having an upbeat 7'2" example to follow.

No one inspires better than a good coach, and I was fortunate to have one of the best during my personal post-stroke training camp. Gregg Popovich checked my improvement weekly. While I was at home but not yet recovered, he came by the house one day at around four in the afternoon. I knew he needed to head to the arena soon for that evening's home game. "Don't you have someplace to be?" I said. He replied sincerely, "What we do on the court is just entertainment. What you're doing is what's really important." Talk about inspiring! I probably walked four times that day.

Recently, more than a year after my stroke, I saw Pop in the locker room. Being the consummate coach that he is, he was still checking on me. "You doing okay now?" he said.

"I'm doing well, Coach. Sixty push-ups a day now," I said.

"Good. Now get the heck out of here," he said in his most intimidating voice. Sympathy time was over. I knew then that I was healed.

I remember turning to my wife once, during the summer I was rehabbing at home, to tell her that Russ Bookbinder was coming by. Russ works twenty-five hours a day but took time to come see the former "Down in Front" guy.

One miserable day, I was walking in the rain, wearing a brown trash bag with head and armholes poked out. I was trying fiercely to keep my right leg from locking at the knee. It unnerved me; I was losing heart. Right then, my cell phone rang. I answered it, and a booming voice said, "All right, all right, all right!" I knew immediately who it was. Red McCombs, the self-made billionaire who became a hero to San Antonio when he helped prevent the team from being sold, was calling all the way from Minnesota just to say hello. Evidently the pending sale of his Vikings could wait. He called long distance to check on my progress.

I was on the stationary bike, working hard. Boxer James Leija called on my cell phone. He just had to know how I was doing. He and I have done many videos together, and we caught up. When I hung up, I pedaled harder.

My dad taught me many things, but one lesson stood out. He told me early and often, "If you want to soar like an eagle, don't hang around with the turkeys." At some point I realized I was truly surrounded by eagles. All these great people are from vastly different fields. But they all have that "go get 'em" enthusiasm for what they do.

They helped me to see that the end of my court career did not necessarily have to mean the end of my story. They gave me the courage to face the future.

Afterword

I was told, long ago, that I'd never make it in acting with my crooked teeth. So I saved up my pennies and got braces in my mid-twenties—which involved two surgeries, having my jaw deliberately broken, and living with my mouth wired shut for forty-nine days.

While I was still in the hospital after one of these procedures, my agent called to say that I'd been selected to star opposite Shelley Winters in a movie. My response took the classic bad news–good news form: I'd have to pass on this big break due to the recent reengineering of my face, but the resulting improved appearance would surely make me more marketable in the future.

I did emerge with a pretty smile. But I almost immediately stumbled onto the Coyote gig, wearing a mask for the next twenty-one years of my performing career. Audiences never saw my face.

Even from behind that mask, I always approached my work in sports entertainment as theater. After the stroke forced me to retire so abruptly from the hardwood stage, I eventually returned to theater, with a five-week run of *Damn Yankees* at the San Pedro Playhouse. My role was both a test—to see how much of a recovery I'd made—and a coda to my career as a performer.

I found myself approaching theater from a sports angle. I didn't want to let my teammates—fellow actors in the troupe—down, so I practiced relentlessly. I struggled to figure out how to hold my right leg so that its uncontrollable shaking, a legacy of the stroke, wouldn't be noticeable on stage. I worked hard to memorize my lines as soon as I could, because I knew my short-term memory had been impaired by the illness.

The parallels to the world of sports entertainment didn't end there. Actors are just as competitive as athletes, a truth I relearned when a colleague took my early progression to "off book" as a challenge to learn his lines ahead of schedule, too. Not only that, just like a skate save in a hockey game, I would sometimes improvise to cover for a fellow actor who got temporarily lost on stage. And I got an assist when it was my turn to goof up my lines; someone would save me. Applause is another version of the scoreboard. Whether it's for an audience of 300 or for a crowd of 30,000, the game plan is the same: just plain entertain.

While I was auditioning to play Mr. Applegate, the casting director asked if I had any special skills. Only a year before I could have replied, "Well, I can do a back flip and a soft shoe, and I can hold myself out horizontally from a pole. I can even walk on my hands from the stage to my car." But I had to admit that those skills were gone, never to return.

I went out for the role to prove to myself that even in my compromised physical state I could sing and do physical comedy. My arms and legs might not be the same, but my entertainer blood was flowing fine. I not only got the part; I also received a Globe Award for best lead actor in a musical from the Alamo Theater Arts Council.

Like many performers, there was no single day, back in my twenties, when I suddenly thought, "I want to be an NBA mascot." There was no plan, no blueprint. And yet my career as a mascot came as no surprise to those who know me: entertaining is my calling. My early theater roles were a preamble to my constitutional work as Coyote; one fed the other.

The other day a woman walked up to me and said she really enjoyed my performing. I figured she was talking about the Coyote—something I've grown to appreciate over the years. I thanked her and told her it was fun.

"You lightened up the day for me and my family," she said. "You truly are a funny man."

I thanked her again.

"I've seen *Damn Yankees* three times in New York," she went on. "And I have to tell you, your portrayal of Applegate was by far the best I've seen."

She was talking about my work on the stage. I was exhilarated.

It was then that I knew I was more actor than athlete. Now the circle felt complete: theater to sports and back to theater. I was born to perform.